Antonio Evaristo Morales-Pita, PhD has worked as a university professor for fifty-six years in Cuba, Mexico, and the USA, where he has been the recipient of numerous national awards. He has written and published eleven books. In the US, he self-published *Havana-Merida-Chicago (A Journey to Freedom)*, 2500 sold copies, and *Gladys, My Unforgettable Love*. Austin Macauley has published *Is It Possible to Inspire Anyone? Is It Always Fun to Travel Abroad?* and *Grit + Tenacity + Proactiveness (Pulling the Bull by the Horns)*. He is an inspirational speaker promoting his books in colleges, universities, factories, and business firms. He has been an official contributor in newspapers and journals. He can speak, write, and read in Spanish, English, Russian, Italian and French.

In memory to my mother, Siria,

Who exerted a considerable influence on my pedagogic, scientific, and writing career.

To the indelible remembrance of my wife, Gladys,

Who transmitted and made me learn the deep feeling of empathy in its deepest human meaning.

To my two children, Rosita and Tonito,

Whose lives and performances materialize my dreams and aspirations as a father.

Antonio Evaristo
Morales-Pita, PhD

CAN LOVE AND TALENTS SURVIVE OPPOSITE POLITICAL AND ECONOMIC ENVIRONMENTS?

AUSTIN MACAULEY PUBLISHERS™

LONDON • CAMBRIDGE • NEW YORK • SHARJAH

Ordering Information
Quantity sales: Special discounts are available on quantity purchases by corporations, associations, and others. For details, contact the publisher at the address below.

Publisher's Cataloging-in-Publication data
Morales-Pita, PhD, Antonio Evaristo
Can Love and Talents Survive Opposite Political and Economic Environments?

ISBN 9798889104421 (Paperback)
ISBN 9798889104438 (ePub e-book)

Library of Congress Control Number: 2023918104

www.austinmacauley.com/us

First Published 2024
Austin Macauley Publishers LLC
40 Wall Street, 33rd Floor, Suite 3302
New York, NY 10005
USA

mail-usa@austinmacauley.com
+1 (646) 5125767

Table of Contents

Introduction   **9**

Chapter I: Comparative Analysis of Chaotic Situations in Cuba and the United States According to the Author's Experience   **15**

Chapter II: Political, Social and Economic Analysis of Capitalist and Communist Countries in Developed and Developing Countries   **26**

Chapter III: Talents, Gifts, or Virtues   **52**

Chapter IV   **75**

4.1 My First Love: My Mother (Siria Pita Allende)   *75*

4.2 My Second Love: My Wife (Gladys)   *83*

4.3 The Interaction Between Mother And Son   *90*

4.4 The Interaction Between Husband and Wife   *95*

4.5 The Interaction Between My Two Loves   *103*

Introduction

During the last three decades, the world has experienced astounding events, such as the fall of the Soviet Union, the creation of the European Union, the rise of China (combining left political system with market economy principles), the changeability of left and right-wing government in Latin America, as well as the transformation of internal and external patterns of American political leaders during the twenty-first century. Are people sure of which is the best political system? Do they understand why Brazil presidents went from left-wing governments that collapsed under corruption, and now the president is right-wing and experiencing corruption? Why Cubans and Venezuelan people, experiencing terrible economic, political, and social situations have not been able to defeat the inefficient and corrupt governments? How is it possible for a small developing country such as Uruguay to be internationally considered a full democracy while the developed United States (one of the most powerful countries of the world) is classified as flawed democracy?

Where can people find explanations for these events? How can they make up their minds and choose the best political system? Just continue reading this book, and you will know.

The author of this book summarizes special characteristics, which allows him to navigate contradictory political systems, such as being a graduate of Marxist economy in Cuba (1967), a master's in mathematics applied to economics in Scotland (1971), and having two doctorates in economics in Ukraine (1982–1990). How could he be a believer in Castro's communism in Cuba from 1959 to 1990 and a disbeliever as of 1991? A professor of environmental economics in Mexico (1993–1996) and a professor of capitalist economics as of 1996 in the US, as well as an extensive traveler of Europe, American and Latin American countries, Australia, East Asia, and Dubai as of 2004.

He has lived in developing and developed right and left-wing countries. He has suffered hunger and fullness, scarcity and surplus of food and medicines, inflation, and deflation, being religious and atheist, experienced abundance and scarcity, uncertainty and peace of mind, respect and disrespect, achievement, and frustration, to fall and to stand up. He is a writer who attempts to teach the readers the contents of his books.

This author believes that it is important to narrate, in an attempted pedagogical way, how he has been affected by living under opposite political systems. It is also important to explain 'how using his talents, and supported by two extraordinary women – he could become one of the first Marxist economists in Cuba, the first masters of science in the University of Havana, one of three Cubans holding two doctorates in Economics, the recipient of multiple awards as a professor and scholar in Cuba, one of the first Cuban economists receiving the award of Cátedra Patrimonial de Excelencia of the Mexican government and the only Cuban-born professor able to receive the Excellence in Teaching Award of DePaul University'.

The main objective of this book is to show how the command economy (also known as socialist or communist) differs from the market economy (also known as capitalist) from political, economic, and social standpoints through the example of a highly qualified Cuban scientist who so far has lived for decades in developing and developed market economy and command economy countries.

This author has resided as a student and faculty in Cuba, the United States, Great Britain, the Soviet Union, Mexico, and as a tourist in all European, North American, almost all Latin American countries, as well as Australia, New Zealand, Singapore, Malaysia, Dubai, Iceland, Patagonian countries, Morocco, Uzbekistan, and Dubai. This extensive world travel is unusual for a Cuban who had never been a member of the Cuban government or worked in the diplomatic sphere; curiously enough, it was based on his passion for studying, learning, and spreading knowledge as a professor.

Another very important and interesting aspect of this book is that it establishes the talents of this man's two big loves – his mother and his second wife, as important and influential contributors in developing his behavior in the politico-socio-economic environment in which his life has so far taken place.

The author believes that this book can clarify the differences between both diametrically opposite political systems and emphasize the importance of love and passion under the influence of this multilateral context.

Under the circumstances, the author remembers and meditates about a starting transcendental moment in his life by the middle of the 1970s when his fiancée at that time, Gladys, recommended that he read Victor Hugo's book *Les Miserables*. The deep and extensive effect of reading this extraordinary book helped him understand the close relationship between the social, political, and economic circumstances surrounding a human being, and that individual's performance in life. The book starts with the apparently insignificant fact of one hungry young man (Jean Valjean) who steals a piece of bread from a bakery and its repercussions on the robber's life under the stressful political situation of the French bourgeois revolution of the eighteenth century. The book narrates the honest life of an empathic young man who faces the relentless persecution of a police officer – Javert – who persists on several occasions to put him in jail. The curious characteristic of the book is that Valjean escapes from jail and on several occasions then leads an honest and empathic life, helping people survive poverty, like Fantine (a prostitute) and her daughter, Cosette, whose happiness becomes Valjean's one of the main objectives in life. Valjean helps humanity in its fight against misery. The book shows several types of monetary and sentimental misery, including the unfair and pernicious persecution of a decent man. The opposite human standpoints between Valjean and Javert exemplifies the extreme consequences of being unfairly demanding. Javert obtains brief victories by jailing Valjean, who manages to escape repeatedly.

At the end of the book, Valjean – after achieving Cosette's happiness – decides to deliver himself to Javert. At that moment, the relentless officer understands how unfair he has been with Valjean and decides to take his own life by throwing himself into the Seine River. In conclusion, this book shows the contraposition of different types of human misery in the context of given political, social and economic situations, in France in the eighteenth century.

To read and to meditate about the content of *Les Miserables* helped the author to humanize his pedagogic approach, and to stop punishing lazy and procrastinating students without any empathic feelings for them. He became a better professor because he was able to combine pedagogic rigor with compassionate human nature. Inspired by reading *Les Miserables*, the author decided to write *Havana-Merida-Chicago (A Journey to Freedom)*, whose content is to analyze a Cuban couple's life escaping from communism from a developing capitalist country in Latin America traveling to developed and developing capitalist and communist countries in Europe and landing in America. Once the author achieved the zenith of this scientific, personal, and loving experience, he became recipient of the Excellence in Teaching Award at DePaul University, accompanied by his extraordinary most significant other. He also felt the need to write about the impact of different socio-politico-economic circumstances on the human and noble feeling of fighting to be free.

Then, with the precedence in mind – at the beginning of his eighth decade – the author made the decision of writing this book, which is divided into four sections: CHAPTER I contains an analytic summary of chaotic situations in Cuba and the United States, in which he had personally participated. CHAPTER II is a comparison of the political, social, and economic advantages and disadvantages existing between the market and the command economies, and the social democracy according to his international scholarly and personal experience, in developing and developed countries, especially during the last half of the twentieth and the first two decades of the twentieth centuries. CHAPTER III explains in depth what is meant by each one of this author's seven talents: reading and writing, pedagogy, tenacity, learning foreign languages, traveling around the world, singing, and being empathetic. CHAPTER IV explains how these talents are related to those of the two women who had considerably influenced the performance of his life – his mother and his second wife.

Chapter I
Comparative Analysis of Chaotic Situations in Cuba and the United States According to the Author's Experience

"Markets weed out inefficient practices, but only when no one has sufficient power to manipulate them."

Ha-Joon Chang

"History is not like some individual person who uses men to achieve its ends, history is nothing but the action of men in pursuit of their ends."

Karl Marx

"Practical men, who believe themselves to be quite exempt from any intellectual influences, are usually the slaves of some defunct economist."

John Maynard Keynes

Today is March 14th, 2020. The president of the United States of America announced an Emergency Situation. A new political, social, and economic situation is taking place in the country. This is not the first time that the author has lived through dangerously catastrophic worldwide situations. Further down, he will enumerate and briefly describe, in a table, the catastrophic conditions experienced by him while living in Cuba with a view to compare them with the one that we as Americans are facing now.

Table# 1:

Chaotic situation	Political implication	Economic implication
Fidel Castro's army defeats Batista's right-wing dictatorship – January 1959. The oppression of the people during Batista's times appears to be over. Temporary peace.	The victory against a capitalist tyrant transfers Cuba into a socialist developing country. The Cuban people was informed that the revolution was humanist, not communist.	The economy is poor, at first there were certain social —rather than economic— improvements, but a latent opposite situation comes slowly to the surface.
Missile crisis ensues between the United States and the Cuban governments – October 1962.	Tension between leaders of opposite political sides almost generates World War III.	Despite Soviet support, a world war threatens to harm the weak Cuban economy.
The Ten Million Tons of Sugar fails - July. 1970. This was an assumed future achievement of Cuban socialism	Socialism suffers defeat against the superiority of capitalism.	The Cuban economy is seriously harmed due to useless dilapidation of economic resources, including the Soviet subsidy.
Relations between Cuba and the Soviet Union falter - 1990	Socialism cannot achieve the promised "luminous" future of the Cuban people. Finally, I am deceived by the real and ominous dictatorial	The euphemistically called "Special Period" is brought to life, with a huge economic and food crisis that has, so far, not been ended.

	behavior of Fidel Castro.	
Stagnation, generalized backward movement, internal opposition keeps on growing despite ferocious repression, widespread decline in Cuba. 1991. Special period.	Feelings of disenchantment, sadness, and lack of hope prevail in most of the Cuban population. It is impossible to substitute the defeated Cuban socialism due to reinforced repression.	The economy is now dependent on Hugo Chavez's "generosity". The economy remains poor. Political leaders resist losing their privileges by accepting radical changes
I live in Mexico as leader of environmental groups and as a professor, representing the Cuban Higher Education Ministry – September 1993 to July 1995	To live in a developing capitalist country enriches my understanding of political economy of capitalism, especially freedom of expression in opposite parties.	In Cuba the economic situation stays the same (the existence of two currencies worsens the people's internal division). My personal situation notably improves.
I visit Cuba for a week (My mother is seriously ill) and I am deprived of my passport. I am inside the gigantic jail of Cuba. July 1995 to January 1996.	My disenchantment is definite. I break up with the repressive regime. My future return to Cuba turns out to be impossible.	My economic situation gets worse. Thanks to Gladys my passport is returned. I am allowed to leave Cuba for 2 months (Jan. 1996) or I will be sought out.
I decide to defect to Mexico, but without receiving asylum status; I	I physically break from communism's chains; and start to	Infinite financial, educational, and scientific possibilities are wide open to me. I

knock at the door of the American Consulate in Merida. – March to April 1996	be a free man in the United States.	start to be the owner of my destiny.
I received political asylum status in the US and live in a Chicago shelter with my wife. At the beginning I live in a hostile social environment in a dangerous area threatened by gangs. We receive a solid economic help without having to pay for rent, food, transportation in Chicago. I receive an important help in filling out documentation for asylum from Father Morales, the manager of La Posada. May to July 1996	I live among Hispanics supporting my wife's while she learns English and gets acquainted with the American way of life. I met unknown American friends and Hispanic leaders who give me considerable physical and psychological support. We survive living in Humboldt Park and learn what it means to be unemployed receiving financial help from the government. Used to work so hard, I am uncomfortable to receiving monetary compensation without working. We receive our social security numbers.	Our savings during our stay in Mexico, and the habitational and financial support received from Casa Central, allow us to prosper and become financially responsible and to enjoy life as free citizens of the most powerful economic country in the world. For the first time we receive credit cards and open checking accounts.

The author's life has given him so far – up to June 2020 – an opportunity to have firsthand experience in analyzing how deep is the impact of politico-economic governmental measures on the populations.

Table# 1 briefly summarizes some of the most important chaotic and tense situations experienced by the author in Cuba, Mexico, the Soviet Union and the U.S.

Each one of the components in this table represents one chaotic situation that the author has undergone during his adult life, not only in Cuba but also in Great Britain, the former Soviet Union, Mexico, and the United States. Living in various opposing political, social, and economic systems has had a direct impact on the romantic whereabouts from which he comes from and where he met the two big loves of his life. In other words, this context talks about how the love life of a person is influenced by the previously mentioned systems. Reading the table and meditating on possible answers to these questions allows the reader to understand the deep impact that both loves had in the formation and success that the author experienced during his times in Cuba and abroad.

Invest some minutes in the analysis of each chaotic situation. While reading the book, you will be able to understand the role that each one of his loves played in the formation of this writer from a deeply human standpoint amidst different political, economic, and social environments.

These critical chaotic situations were created by the stubbornness, bullheadedness, bloody mindedness, egoism, passionate love for the power of one man, who was able to cheat and to betray, not only the Cuban people, but also leaders of other Latin American countries – like Venezuela, Nicaragua, Bolivia, Ecuador, and Chile, who have expressed open veneration for him. He never went to international trials at La Haya (The Hague) in the Netherlands to be judged for his multiple crimes and assassinations, including some of the legitimate natural leaders of the Cuban revolution. He died of natural causes in his bed. He eliminated the celebration of Christmas for decades (lying about the real causes) and persecuted the church. He was like a god, denying any sort of competition, which was repressed and continues to be repressed violently after his death.

For more than a decade, the Cuban people's health appeared to be good. Healthcare was free of charge for the whole country, although, as usual in every communist government – there were shortages of medicines, food, toilet paper, and medical equipment... which, as a result, had to be imported. The main reason is that the demand was always greater than the supply due to the economic inefficiency of the command economy in relation to the market economy. The good side of this healthcare situation in Cuba was that the prices of the medicines were low – within reach for most of the population – and that visits to all doctors and hospitals were free. The previous information was valid until the Soviet subsidy to the price of Cuban raw sugar ended. The population was always informed by the press that the reason for these economic measures were attributed to the superiority of socialism in relation to the market economy. The real reason was never made public to the population. The Special Period revealed the inefficiency inherent to the command economy. Now the guilty one was the American embargo, which was always less significant than the internal embargo exerted by the Cuban governments on its people. The very name of the period was false. The word 'especial' is usually applied to something valuable, estimated as good. The right denomination of the period should have been The Shortage or Scarcity period. The Soviet subsidy was replaced by the Venezuelan, but the economy as such was always considered by the Cuban government and treated to be of secondary importance in relation to politics.

I will now summarize the dangerous and critical situations closely related to the healthcare issues the country where I was born is facing; I will gather up the elements known to me now to reach a generalization. Suddenly in the month of January 2020, a new, totally unknown, virus is reported in China, where it showed an incredibly fast pace in spreading, affecting thousands of people, especially among those in the so-called third age. In a matter of days, the virus reaches Japan, South Korea, and Europe. After some days, it was discovered in the United States and in many other countries. The new virus elicits questions around such topics as: a) its origin; b) the reason for its fast spread; c) the types of testing that ought to be developed to determine the presence of the virus in the human body; d) the necessary measures to fight against the sickness; e) the capacity of our hospitals and the volume of necessary equipment like ventilators required to fight a sickness that might become an epidemic.

It is just a coincidence that at the same moment as the appearance and contagion of the new virus, our country is facing an acute political competition, which is deeply dividing the country in two opposing right and left-wing positions. We are in a period of holding political meetings (with concentrations of thousands of people) that – unfortunately – facilitates the spreading of epidemics.

Our country has a highly respected scientific and medical stature, prestigious hospitals at international levels, but, are the capacity of our hospitals and of the necessary equipment such as ventilators – both governmental and privately owned – prepared to treat the huge number of patients affected by this pandemic? Our medical teams and hospitals do have experience treating previous viruses like Ebola and the flu, but these are different from the one that has entirely occupied our media and news agencies since the month of February 2020. It should be borne in mind that our healthcare system is not an example for the world, given the amount of people without health insurance, and the high cost of prescriptions.

This problem needs to be solved through the direct participation of the government because it is a national crisis, unrelated to the political affiliations dividing our people. Bipartisanship should not be an issue under a critical situation like this. We need a president who is able to: 1) listen and understand opinions different from his own, 2) assume responsibility for past hesitations and mistakes, and be willing to apologize whenever needed in order to lead the country in the right direction, 3) base his decisions on scientific data, not good wishes or his imagination, 4) be calm and intelligent an avoid contradicting himself because confusion fosters panic in times like this, 5) consult and support the scientific development of our scholars and professional specialists, 6) respect and avoid insulting qualified individuals, who disagree with him, 7) get rid of advisors who merely praise him to satisfy his ego, which distract him from concentrating on what is good for the people who chose him.

Since Gladys and the author arrived in the United States in April 1996, they have been able to overcome some difficult moments – which were incomparably easier than the ones they went through in either Cuba or Mexico. For example, during the economic recession that took place during Bush's second four-year presidency, they never stopped eating, buying clothes, owning our home, working as professors, or even traveling abroad. Both became American citizens in July 2004 – exactly eight years after their arrival in Chicago from Mexico. Here they both realized not only the American dream, but also fulfilled all their aspirations, and even some which they had never thought about, like traveling around the world.

We, as Americans, are now facing a period of uncertainty with the coronavirus surge and middle-term election in November 2022 and the presidential elections approaching in November 2024. We are mentally prepared to overcome the forthcoming recession and we expect periods of recovery and hope that we never experienced before becoming American citizens.

Section two: to show how the Command Economy (also known as socialist or communist) differs from the Market Economy (also known as capitalist), from economic, politic, and social standpoints through the example of a highly qualified Cuban scientist who so far has lived for seven decades in developing and developed Market

Economy countries as well as developing and developed Command Economy countries.

Given the radical changes taking place in the world, such as the fall of the Soviet Union, the creation of the European Union, the rise of China –combining left political system with market economy principles – the changeability of left and right wings government in Latin America, the international trade agreements, as well as the transformation of internal and external patterns of American political leaders during the twenty-first century, this author believes that it is important to narrate – in a pedagogical way – how he has been affected by living under opposite political systems in different parts of the world.

Let us see now how developed and developing capitalist countries have been doing as far as political, social, and economic parameters are concerned.

Chapter II
Political, Social and Economic Analysis of Capitalist and Communist Countries in Developed and Developing Countries

"The time has surely gone in which economists could analyze in detail two individuals exchanging nuts for berries on the edge of the forest and then feel that their analysis of the process of exchange was complete, illuminating though this analysis may be in certain respects."

Ronald H. Coase

"We have this culture of financialization. People think they need to make money with their savings rather than with their own business. So you end up with dentists who are more traders than dentists. A dentist should drill teeth and use whatever he does in the stock market for entertainment."

Nassim Nicholas Taleb

"Economics is only considered the dismal science because economists are so often called on to clean up after innumerate politicians."

Ted Seay

The political indicators to be analyzed are index of corruption index of freedom and index of democracy.

Table # 2: Index of Corruption

Country	2019	2015	2013	Place
DEVELOPED CAPITALIST				
UNITED KINGDOM	77	81	76	12
CANADA	77	83	81	12
AUSTRALIA	77	79	85	12
JAPAN	73	75	69	20
USA	69	76	73	23
SOUTH KOREA	59	56	56	39
DEVELOPED SOCIAL DEMOCRACIES				
DENMARK, WHICH IS NUMBER ONE	87	91	91	1
SWEDEN	85	89	89	4
SWITZERLAND	85	86	89	4
NORWAY	84	87	86	7
DEVELOPING CAPITALISTS				
URUGUAY	71	74	72	21
CHILE	67	70	72	26
COSTA RICA	56	55	53	44
ECUADOR	38	32	35	93
COLOMBIA	37	37	36	96
PERU	35	36	38	101
PANAMA	101	72	102	101
BRAZIL	35	38	43	106
BOLIVIA	31	34	34	123
MEXICO	29	30	34	130
NICARAGUA	22	27	28	161
VENEZUELA	16	17	20	173
SEMI-DEVELOPED CAPITALIST OR COMMUNIST				
CUBA	48	53	46	60
HUNGARY	44	51	54	70
CHINA	41	37	39	80
INDIA	41	38	36	80
RUSSIA	28	29	28	137
NORTH KOREA	17	08	08	172

From analyzing table# 2, the author has arrived to the following conclusions:

1. The third group (Social Democracy) concentrates the countries classified in the group of least corruption with general classification between 1 and 7, and consequently the largest numbers going from 84 to 91.

2. The first group (developed capitalist countries) includes countries with the second smallest percentage of corruption. It calls attention to the fact that the United States occupies the twenty-third place in corruption while the United Kingdom, Canada, Australia, and Japan show better results in controlling corruption.

3. The second group (developing capitalist countries) is made of countries with the third smallest percentage of corruption in which only three countries (Uruguay, Chile and Costa Rica) show satisfactory results. Five of them – Ecuador, Brazil, Bolivia, Nicaragua, Venezuela – can be considered to have been strongly linked and influenced by the Cuban government (whose economy had always been dependent on foreign countries like the United States, the Soviet Union, and Venezuela).

4. The fourth group (semi-develop capitalists or communist) has the most corrupted results. Except for India, which is the largest democracy in the world, the remaining five countries either have been or still are communist countries. It is a mixture

of communist or semi-communist countries (like Cuba, China, Russia, and North Korea).

Table # 3: Index of corruption between the US and Uruguay from 2012 to 2019

19 18 17 16 15 14 13 12

		19			18			17			16			15			14			13			12
23	United States	69	▼ 2	71	▼ 4	75	▲ 1	74	▼ 2	76	▲ 2	74	▲ 1	73	—	73							
21	Uruguay	71	▲ 1	70	—	70	▼ 1	71	▼ 3	74	▲ 1	73	—	73	▲ 1	72							

It is interesting to observe that during the last eight years, in the US, there were three years of improvement (2013–2016) few years of worsening (2015, 2017–2019), while in Uruguay, three years of improvement (2012, 2014, 2019) a year of worsening (2015–2016) and two years of same level (2013 and 2017). So, the corruption in Uruguay (developing capitalist country) reported better results than in the US (developed capitalist country).

Uruguay is the least corrupt country in Latin America, which has maintained a relatively low level from 72 to 71, therefore a more stable country, despite being a developing nation. The United States (the largest and richest capitalist country in the world) shows worse results than Uruguay because it went down – which means more corruption indexes – from 73 to 69, especially from 2016 to 2019. The US has traditionally been considered one of the most democratic countries in the world, but this worsening situation in corruption turns out to be alarming and questions the US supremacy in its fight against corruption.

Index of corruption:

The Social Democracy countries concentrate the best numbers, followed by the capitalist developed countries, the third group the developing countries with three exceptions (Uruguay, Costa Rica and Chile); the fourth group include the worst developing counting plus the communist countries.

The second political parameters analyzed in this book are the indexes of freedom and democracy.
https://en.wikipedia.org/wiki/List_of_freedom_indices

Table # 4: Indexes of freedom and democracy

Country	Freedom in the world 2020	220 Index of Economic Freedom	2020 Press Freedom Index	2019 Democracy Index
Australia	free	free	Satisfactory situation	Full democracy
Canada	free	Mostly free	Satisfactory situation	Full democracy
Chile	free	Mostly free	Noticeable problems	Full democracy
Costa Rica	free	Moderately free	Good situation	Full democracy
Denmark	free	Mostly free	Good situation	Full democracy
Iceland	free	Mostly free	Satisfactory situation	Full democracy
Ireland	free	free	Good situation	Full democracy
Luxembourg	free	Mostly free	Satisfactory situation	Full democracy
Netherlands	free	Mostly free	Good situation	Full democracy
New Zealand	free	Free	Good situation	Full democracy
Norway	free	Mostly free	Good situation	Full democracy
Sweden	Free	Mostly free	good situation	Full democracy
Switzerland	free	free	Good situation	Full democracy
United Kingdom	Free	Mostly free	Satisfactory situation	Full democracy
Uruguay	Free	Moderately	Satisfactory situation	Full democracy
Belgium	free	Moderately free	Good situation	Flawed democracy
Brazil	free	Mostly unfree	Noticeable problems	Flawed democracy
Colombia	Partly free	Moderately free	Difficult situation	Flawed democracy
Ecuador	Partly free	Mostly unfree	Noticeable problems	Flawed democracy
El Salvador	Partly free	Moderately free	Noticeable problems	Flawed democracy
Hungary	Partly free	Moderately free	Noticeable problems	Flawed democracy
India	free	Mostly unfree	Difficult situation	Flawed democracy
Mexico	Partly free	Mostly unfree	Difficult situation	Flawed democracy

Panama	free	Moderately free	Noticeable problems	Flawed democacy
Peru	free	Moderately free	Noticeable problems	Flawed democacy
Singapore	Partly free	free	Very serious situation	Flawed democacy
United States	Free	Mostly free	Satisfactory situation	Flawed democacy
Guatemala	Partly free	Moderately free	Difficult situation	Hybrid regime
Bolivia	Partly free	Repressed	Difficult situation	Hybrid regime
China	Not free	Mostly unfree	Very serious situation	Authoritarian regime
Cuba	Not free	repressed	Very serious situation	Authoritarian regime
Korea North	Not free	repressed	Very serious situation	Authoritarian regime
Nicaragua	Not free	Mostly unfree	Difficult situation	Authoritarian regime
Russia	Not free	Moderately free	Difficult situation	Authoritarian regime
Venezuela	Not free	repressed	Difficult situation	Authoritarian regime

Table # 5: Summarizing above countries by political and democratic regime categories

political classification regime	Social democracy	Developed capitalist	Developing capitalist	communist
Full democracy	8	4	3	0
Flawed democracy	0	2	10	0
Hybrid	0	0	2	0
Authoritarian	0	0	2	3

An interesting conclusion of this table is that all social democracy countries are considered or classified inside the full democracy category. Two thirds of the developed capitalist countries enjoy a full democracy regime, while one-third are classified as flawed democracies. The developing capitalist countries can be found in the four categories, although they are majority in the flawed democracy regime. All communist countries are classified as authoritarian.

The analysis of the preceding table indicates that: fifteen countries are classified with a full democracy regime, except for the communist ones. Twelve countries (classified inside the flawed democracy regimes) out of which two are developed (the United States and Singapore) and ten developing capitalist countries in Latin America. Two countries (both developing Latin American countries) are classified with a hybrid regime. Finally, five countries are classified as authoritarian, three of them in the communist group and two in the developing capitalist group. An interesting conclusion of this table is that all social democracy countries are considered inside the full democracy category. Two thirds of the developed capitalist countries enjoy a full democracy regime, while one-third are classified as flawed democracies. The developing capitalist countries can be found in the four categories, although they are majority in the flawed democracy regime. All communist countries are classified as authoritarian.

Index of Freedom

An interesting conclusion of this table is that all social democracy countries are considered inside the full democracy category. Two thirds of the developed capitalist countries enjoy a full democracy regime, while one-third are classified as flawed democracies. The developing capitalist countries can be found in the four categories, although they are majority in the flawed democracy regime. All communist countries are classified as authoritarian.

Social Indicators.

In this manuscript we are only going to consider the Gini coefficient (income inequality) and the Human Development Index

The Gini coefficient is a number between 0 and 1, where 0 corresponds with perfect equality (where everyone has the same income) and 1 corresponds with perfect inequality (where one person has all the income and everyone else has no income). Income distribution can vary greatly from wealth distribution in a country.

Table # 6: Gini coefficient in 1994, 2008, and 2010 divided by democracy regimes.

Country	World Bank Gini[3]		CIA R/P[4]		CIA Gini[5]	
	%	Year	10%	Year	%	Year
Full democracies						
Australia *	34.4	2014	12.7	1994	30.3	2008
Canada *	33.8	2013	9.5	2000	32.1	2005
Chile o	44.4	2017	32.1	2003	52.1	2009
Costa Rica o	48.0	2018	37.3	2003	50.3	2009
Denmark **	28.7	2017	12.0	2000 est.	24.8	2011 est.
Canada *	33.8	2013	9.5	2000	32.1	2005
France *	31.6	2017	8.3	2004	30.1	2013
Germany **	31.9	2016	6.9	2000	27.0	2006
Iceland **	26.8	2015			28.0	2006
Japan *	32.9	2013	4.5	1993	37.9	2011
Netherlands *	28.5	2017	9.2	1999	25.1	2013

New Zealand					36.2	1997
Norway * *	27.0	2017	6.0	2000	26.8	2010
South Korea*	31.6	2012	5.9	2011	34.1	2015
Sweden * *	, and t28.8	2017	6.2	2000	24.9	2013
Switzerland	32.7	2017	8.9	2000	28.7	2012 est.
United Kingdom *	34.8	2016	13.6	1999	32.4	2012
Uruguay o	39.7	2018	17.9	2003	45.3	2010
FLAWED DEMOCRACIES						
Belgium	27.4	2017	8.3	2000	25.9	2013 est.
Brazil o	46.6	2018	16.3	2013	48.8	2018
Colombia o	50.4	2018	56.3	2008	53.5	2012
Ecuador o	45.4	2018	17.5	2006 Oct.[8]	48.5	2013 Dec.[8]
Hungary **	30.6	2017	5.6	2002	24.7	2009
India *	37.8	2011	8.6	2004	35.1	2011
Mexico o	45.4	2018	24.6	2004	48.3	2008

Peru o	42.8	2018	31.5	2003	45.3	2012
Singapore o			17.3	1998	46.4	2014
United States o	41.4	2016	14.0	2014 est.	47.0	2014
Hybrid Regimes						
Bolivia o	42.2	2018	157.3	2002	46.6	2012
AUTHORITARIAN REGIMES						
China o	38.5	2016	21.8	2004	46.5	2016
Nicaragua o	46.2	2014	15.4	2001	40.5	2010
Russia o	37.5	2018	12.8	2002	42	2012
Venezuela o	46.9	2006	50.3	2003	39.0	2011

*Banco Central** de Uruguay ** Banco Central de Costa Rica *** World *Bank Central de Uruguay o Wikipedia.org Banco Central de Uruguay ** Banco Central de Costa Rica*** World Bank o o National Bureau Statistics of China Notation ** in the twenties; * in the thirties, o in the forty-fifties

It can be seen that : a) the lowest income inequality correspond to the full democracies countries, 47% show indexes in the range 0.20–0.29 to the European social democracies, 35% indexes in the range 0.30–.039 to the developed capitalist countries, and the remaining 17% in the range 0.40–0.50 to the developing Latin American countries; b) the intermediate inequality correspond to the flawed democracies with the majority of the countries range 0.40–0.50, forty percent correspond to developed capitalist countries, two in Europe, two in Asia, and six in the American continent; the two European countries of this group registered income inequalities in the lowest range; c) the authoritarian regimes registered a general intermediate income inequality. It is interesting to note that China and Russia showed improvement between 2012 and 2018, while the two Latin American countries showed the opposite trend.

The Human Development Index

The **Human Development Index (HDI)** is a summary measure of average achievement in key dimensions of **human development**: a long and healthy life, being knowledgeable and have a decent standard of living. The **HDI** is the geometric mean of normalized **indices** for each of the three dimensions. (Taken from Wikipedia.org)

Table # 7: The Human Development Index (HDI) 2017–2018

RANK		COUNTRY	HDI	
2017	Change in rank		2018 data	Change from
rankings	From previous year		(2019 report)	Previous year
1	-	Norway	0.954	+0.02
2	-	Switzerland	0.946	+0.01
3	-	Ireland	0.942	+0.04
4	-	Germany	0.939	+0.02
6	+1	Iceland	0.938	+0.02
6	-1	Australia	0.938	+0.01
8	-1	Sweden	0.937	+0.01
9	-	Singapore	0.935	+0.02
10	-	Netherlands	0.933	+0.03
11	-	Denmark	0.923	+0.01
13	-	Canada	0.922	+0.04
14	-	New Zealand	0.921	+0.02
15	-	United Kingdom	0.920	+0.02
15	-2	United States (flawed democracy)	0.920	+0.02
17	-	Belgium (flawed democracy)	0.919	+0.01
19	-	Japan	0.915	+0.02
22	-	South Korea	0.906	+0.03

26	-	France	0.891	+0.02
42	-	Chile	0.847	+0.01
43	-	Hungary (flawed democracy)	0.845	+0.03
49	-	Russia (authoritarian	0.824	+0.01
57	+1	Uruguay	0.808	+0.02
76	-	Mexico (flawed democracy)	0.767	+0.02
129	-	India (flawed d.)	0.647	+0.02

"Human Development Index Trends, 1990-2017". HDRO (Human Development Report Office) United Nations Development Program. Archived (PDF) from the original on 22 March 2017. Retrieved 14 September 2018.

From the analysis of the table, the full democracies (in particular, the social democratic countries get the best numbers from 0.954 to 0.92, except for Belgium and France, with 0.919 and 0.891) show the best situation in the world. The only full democracy developing capitalists – Chile and Uruguay – reached acceptable HDI numbers of 0.847 and 0.808 respectively.

Table # 8: Economic indicators, GDP, budgetary deficit/GDP, % unemployment and %inflation.

Country	Gdp	Gdp	Gdp	Budget %Gdp	Unemployment 1	Inflation 2 - 3		
	2015 - 2019	2007- 2012	2003 2008	2017	2019	2014	2019	2008- 2013
FULL DEMOCRACIES								
Belgium	1.5	0.4	2.3	-2.1	5.6	8.5	1.4	1.9
Denmark	1.6	-0.9	1.8	-0.6	4.9	6.6	0.8	1.9
France	1.5	0.1	1.8	-3.1	8.4	10.3	1.1	1.5
Germany	1.6	0.7	1.8	0.7	3.8	5.0	1.4	1.5
Hungary	2.5	-1.0	2.8	-2.5	3.4	7.7	3.3	4.1
Italy	0.8	-1.4	1.9	-2.3	9.9	11.7	0.6	2.0
Ireland	3.2	-1.2	3.8	-0.6	4.9	11.9	0.9	0.1
Netherlands	1.8	-0.1	2.7	0.6	4.1	5.8	2.6	2.0
Norway	1.5	0.6	2.7	4.2	3.3	3.5	2.2	1.7
Spain	2.1	-1.0	3.1	-3.3	14	22.1	0.7	1.8
Sweden	2.5	0.9	2.8	0.9	6.6	8.0	1.8	0.9
United Kingdom	2.3	-0.6	2.2	-1.1	3.9	6.1	1.7	3.1
Australia o	2.6	2.7	3.3	-1.7	5.3	6.1	1.6	2.4
Canada o	1.6	1.1	2.4	-2.0	5.6	6.9	1.9	1.5
New Zealand o	3.2 (2018) 2.2 (2019)	0.7	2.2	0.7	4.1	5.8	1.6	2.1
Japan o	1.12	-0.2	1.6	-4.6	2.41	3.6	0.5	-0.4
Chile o	2.4	3.9	4.9	-3.1	7.1	6.7	2.6	2.2
Uruguay	2017 –19	-3.7	8.7	6.5	7.9	8.0	7.9	8
	From 4.6 to 1.3*							
Costa Rica	2017 – 2020 GDP	-5.2	11.9	8.8	2.1	4.52	2.1	4.52

	from 4.2 to 2.9 **							
South Korea o	2.9	2.9	4.2	0.6	4.1	3.5	0.4	2.6
FLAWED DEMOCRACIES								
USA o	2.4	0.8	2.4	-4.6	3.7	6.2	1.8	1.6
Singapore	0.7 – 2.9	4.3	7.0	1.8	4.1	3.7	-0.8	0.6
Mexico	0.3 – 0.2	1.8	3.4	-1.9	3.5	5	2.83	4.2
India`	8.5 -6	6.5	8.7	-6.9	5.57	5.36	9.63	10.6
HYBRID REGIME								
Bolivia	4.8 – 4.2	4.5–5.1	2.7– 6.1	-6.2	3.5	2.3	1.23	2.8
AUTHORITARIAN REGIMES								
Nicaragua	4.7 – - 0.2	5– -5	1 – 5	– 2	6.8	4.5	3.25	3.90
Russia	0.1	1.8	7.0	-2.3	4.6	5.2	4.5	7.7
Venezuela o	12.9	2.0	10.2	-38.1	8.8	7.5	255	28.5
China o o	6.6	9.3	10.9	-4.0	4.3	4.6	2.9	2.6

*Banco Central de Uruguay

** Banco Central de Costa Rica

*** World Bank

Wikipedia.org

National Bureau Statistics of China

The analysis of table# 7 indicates that the GDP growth in: a) the full democracies shows a more stable economic situation as a whole in the social democratic European countries, although it reached smaller growths that in the remaining full democracies b) the flawed democracies experienced similar situations shared by developing and developed countries; c) the authoritarian regimes show two contrasting situations Russia and China experienced drastic reductions, while Nicaragua and Venezuela registered fluctuation results.

It is assumed that up to 3% of the budgetary deficit in relation to the GDP is an indication that the corresponding governments are using adequate fiscal policies, consequently, the full democracies are doing very well, including exceptional performance in the developing countries. Among the flawed democracies, the USA and India show alarming results. The authoritarian regimes show generally acceptable results except for Venezuela.

Unemployment data up to 2019 show descending numbers, although there still are worrying cases like in Spain, Chile, Uruguay, Nicaragua, and Venezuela. During the current Coronavirus crisis in 2020, this indicator should experience alarming increases in the global economy, including that of the United States.

Inflation is not a big problem in the countries included in this analysis, except for Uruguay, India, Russia, and Venezuela.

Concluding the economic analysis, without including the effect of the coronavirus crisis, most of the countries are showing favorable economic results. Although the full democracies register the best situations, followed by the flawed democracies in the capitalist developed and developing countries, and finally by the authoritarian regimes.

Summarizing the political, social, and economic situations of developed and developing capitalist and communist countries, the social democracy countries occupy the best positions in all indicators; they represent a combination of efficient market economy and a reasonable shared participation of the government which respects the rational use of high taxes combined with free high level of education and health care.

The second place is occupied by capitalist countries such as Australia, New Zealand, Great Britain, South Korea, Japan, Iceland, The United States, and Singapore, as well as by three Latin American developing countries, which become an example to follow by the rest of the developing LA countries.

The third place is in the hands of the capitalist developing countries, with fluctuating economic situations of the extreme left or extreme right.

The fourth place corresponds to the communist developing countries such as North Korea, Cuba and the ones that had imitated its system such as Venezuela, Nicaragua, Bolivia, Ecuador, and North Korea. Russia also reports very poor results.

As a professor for more than one decade of the course Operational Research, I can make a comparison of one of the graphs that I explained to my students. It is the following:

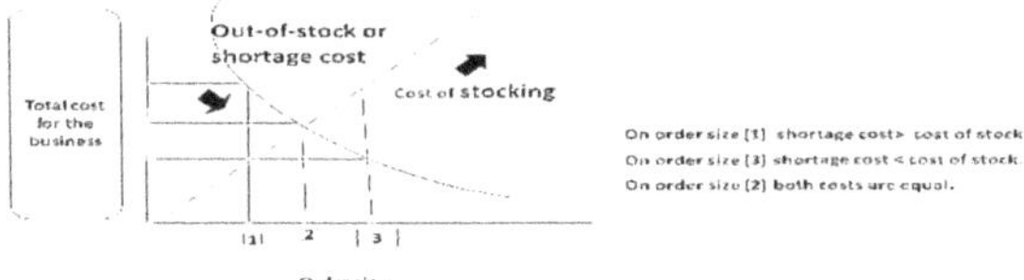

The explanation is quite simple: One businessman supplies one product whose demand is not deterministic, therefore, it is hard for him to exactly calculate its volume during a given period. He faces two opposite costs: the stockholding cost – which prioritizes the satisfaction of the demand of the customer, and the shortage cost – which implies that the customer's demand will not be satisfied in the amount in which he needs it. If the owner of factory keeps in stock large number of products, his stockholding costs will increase, while the shortage costs will go down or even turn to zero (this is point number three); while, on the other hand, if he keeps a relatively small stock of products, his stockholding costs will go down, while the shortage costs will increase (point # 3). The owner's dilemma is that he does not exactly know how much the demand will be, which is supposed to be probabilistic. He needs to run the risk, and his ability as a producer would be to find the average point of coincidence between the demand and the supply of the product with the minimal cost.

In political terms, the intersection point between the stock holding and the shortage costs would be an intermediate political participation of the government, which would imply low level of corruption, income inequality, full democratic country, stable and acceptable GDP growth low levels of unemployment and deficit in the budget in relation to the GDP, and so on. This is attainable, but hard to keep for a long time. The social democracy in European Union countries has proven to be able to keep an acceptable level of balance with ups and downs created by the essence of the creation of the monetary union which establishes free movement of capital, trade and people. During the period 2014 to 2019, the European Union has been able to keep a maximum of 3% in the budgetary deficit of most member countries, and a descending rate of unemployment. The GDP growths are not astounding but systematically acceptable levels in the range 0.5 to 3%.

In political terms, the objective to find an intermediate situation between left and right-wing governments is somewhat equivalent to intertwine acceptable levels of the unemployment, inflation, governmental, and private sector participations. In other words, the satisfaction of the customer and the business owners'.

This author's personal experiences – going through diverse political, social, and economic situations in the four political regime countries, where he had resided – required the acquisition of knowledge acquired during decades of systematic and deep study of economic and social sciences, and his 54 years of teaching as well as the talents partially inherited from his mother and his one-of-a-kind wife, as the readers will learn while reading this book.

The readers may experience different degrees of difficulties in going through the classifications analyzed in this chapter according to their educational preparation and passion for discovering the main varieties of political systems and talents which create the basis for interiorizing and understanding the variety of socio-political systems. This book was written with the intention of providing the required information.

Getting deeper into this interconnection, the lack of interaction starts to be understood if the readers' attention is addressed to the fact that socio-political-economic issues are directly related to human beings' diverse roles in society. The history of the and 20th and 21st centuries identify very harmful leaders such as Adolf Hitler, Benito Mussolini, Joseph Stalin, Vladimir Putin, Anastasio

Somoza, Augusto Pinochet, Porfirio Diaz, Fulgencio Batista, Fidel Castro, Hugo Chavez, and so on. Some of them were initially progressive, supposedly defending their peoples' interests and later they deeply fell in love with power, supposedly for the following reasons: money, fame, and power.

According to google.com, any **power**, money, or influence obtained through illegitimate means can be termed as corruption. It is one of the biggest problems of the world and a huge number of populations in many countries have fallen victim to this menace. In this post, we will try to explain the main causes of corruption in countries all over the world.

In this post, this author will attempt to explain the main causes of corruption in countries all over the world.

While browsing about the reasons for corruption, the author has come across an interesting and relevant paper. According to Hackbrain.net, the main causes of corruption, common in all countries of the world are the following: a) poor financial condition, b) introduction of more regulations – it has become easier for the officials to take a bribe, c) faults in the system (weakness of the legislative and judicial systems), d) **Poor Ethics and Law Development** – Ethics plays an important role in the personality development of any person. It is the ethics which prevents a person from walking on the wrong path. Also, the effective implementation of laws makes it possible to curb corruption at various levels. Without stringent laws, it becomes easier for anyone to adopt illegitimate ways to get his job done, e) the Imbalance between population and natural resources, and, f) lack of political will. One of the main causes of corruption is lack of political will. There is high political instability which further contributes to making it easy to allow corruption.

This author knows that the connection between political, social, and economic issues on one hand, and an analysis of the talents as such on the other – is not easy to grasp. All leaders are human beings with special abilities to address and to attract the attention of multitudes. When Fidel Castro assumed political power in Cuba, he spoke about fostering, not communism, but humanism. Then the author's knowledge about communism was minimal, and humanism was totally unknown to me. So, since the Cuban people had – in the years preceding 1959 – been subject to an open capitalist dictatorship, we needed a change and Fidel Castro's first year in power appeared to be promising for a better future. Some Cuban people were unpleasantly surprised by Fidel Castro's public announcement. A couple of days before the main invasion force of Cubans, opposed to the Cuban government residing in Miami, landed on the beach at Playa Giron in April 1961 – that the American government couldn't accept that Fidel Castro himself had introduced socialism 90 miles away from the US. I was utterly confused because he didn't talk about humanism, but socialism. I felt cheated, but again ignored what socialism was about. I wondered: "Would it be better than Batista's capitalist dictatorship?"

After April 1961, and the declaration of socialism in Cuba, an avalanche of socialist, Marxist, and Leninist literature invaded Havana and the most important Cuban cities. I was forced to enroll in the career of Marxist economics at the University of Havana. (The reader is referred to my book *Havana-Merida-Chicago (A Journey to Freedom)* for a better understanding of the political situation in Cuba in the decade of the sixties). The Cuban original communists were happy. The Catholic Church was persecuted. The revolutionary Cubans were not supposed to attend church. My first marriage took place in 1963 dressed up in military custom outside of a church. Christmas was eliminated in the 1960s until 1997, when the government declared Christmas a holiday in honor of John Paul's Second upcoming visit to Cuba in 1998.

There is a famous phrase from Jose Marti, a Cuban nationalist, poet, philosopher, essayist, journalist, translator, professor, and publisher, who is considered a Cuban national hero because of his role in the liberation of his country from the Spanish rule.

One very important and transcendental Marti's phrase is the following: "Socialist ideology, like so many others, has 2 main dangers. One stems from confused and incomplete readings of foreign texts, and the other from the arrogance and hidden rage of those who, to climb in the world, pretend to be frantic defenders of the helpless so as to have shoulders on which to stand."

Another one of his phrases is very close to my heart because it deals with education. Here it is: "To educate is to give man the keys to the world, which are independence and love, and to give him strength to journey on his own, light of step, a spontaneous and free being."

As I get more involved in educational matters, the topic of talents acquires a larger importance in this book.

Starting from the following chapters, the emphasis of the book is to open the door to learning about talents, taking the author's and his wife's lives to exemplify the impact of tenacity, courage, and intelligence in the human couple.

Get ready to discover means of achieving success using your talents. You are about to grow intellectually and to be better prepared to understand and to make good decisions in the realm of your intellectual skills. The readers are invited to open their intellects and brain powers about the role of talents in their brains.

Food for Thought

1. The readers are suggested to evaluate – among the parameters or indicators analyzed in this chapter – which are the three most important ones in the context of political, social and economics environments through which the author had so far lived.
2. Have the presented above statistics helped the readers to deduct the main differences between countries classified as social democracy, developed, developing, and communist countries?
3. It would also be useful for the readers to establish an order of preference between full, and flawed democracies, hybrid, and authoritarian regimes.
4. Have the readers previously meditated about which are their most transcendental talents?
5. The readers are recommended to think about their natural aptitude or skills before starting chapter III.

Chapter III
Talents, Gifts, or Virtues

"Talent wins games, but teamwork and intelligence win championships."

Michael Jordan

"Winning takes talent, to repeat takes character."

John Wooden

"Doing easily what others find difficult is talent; doing what is impossible with talent is genius."

Henri Frederic Amiel

In this book – in general terms – the author will use the words "talents" or "gifts" or "virtues" to define special skills human beings have been able to handle, to manage, to perform or to possess to successfully start, execute, perform, and conclude tasks, assignments, or even spontaneous actions or duties.

- Talent for reading and writing. This virtue can be inborn, acquired, or – if the parents are fans of reading and writing – be stimulated at home.

Parents can instill the habit of reading in their offspring by buying and reading age-appropriate books to their children, to show them the joy of learning through reading. Another way is parents' direct participation in their children's education by visiting their children's schools, talking to their teachers, and participating in parent-teacher meetings. If the children observe that their parents are really interested in their studies, a healthy interrelationship of respect and admiration can be developed within the family. Children will feel that their education is important for mom and dad.

The vocation for writing is likely to appear after children have learned to read and write, which are necessary skills for future stages of education. If they live in a home where there is love between parents and in relation to them, it is possible for children to accept home as a good place for studying, doing homework and exchanging ideas with their parents. If mom and/or dad encourage children to write paragraphs, letters, and small essays, if they read them and offer feedback, the parent-child interrelation may be fantastic. If parents can undertake some sort of study themselves, the general environment of study will fill the house with good will and love. Bear in mind that boys imitate their fathers, while girls generally imitate their mothers. If parents observe that the professional orientation manifested by their children goes in a different direction than their own, so be it! He/she may give advice, but the child's vocation is his/her own; it should be respected and encouraged.

The inborn writer feels the need to communicate something, to write down ideas, to express wishes, hopes, dreams, and aspirations, to describe, to project and to talk about ideas, to put them in writing, to show writing to their parents, to receive feedback from them. A child needs to feel support and encouragement from the most important people in their lives. If a child approaches his/her parents and asks for an opinion about the quality of the writing, that child is showing confidence in their parents' opinion and good intentions. Of course, there are children who do not feel a vocation for writing and do not feel motivated to do so unless it is a part of their homework in school. Some children may be encouraged, others may not. The inborn writer realizes himself/herself when – on a piece of paper or in a copybook – he/she writes down his/her thoughts, feelings, concepts, or any type of information. He/she must enjoy what he/she is doing, review or modify it until he/she feels satisfied with he/she has done. The child must be demanding about the quality of his/her creation, and their parents may help him/her achieve his/her purpose by giving insights and opinions, always keeping in mind ways to encourage him/her to follow the right track. Parents can be wonderful mentors. If they are not professionally or technically qualified, they might ask for help from the school or institution where their offspring are studying. But it is recommended parents ask for the child's approval, or at least opinion before they do so. It is good for him/her to be consulted to have his/her point of view taken into consideration.

From the author's vocation as a writer manifested since he was studying in primary school, and having published eight books, and written three additional manuscripts in the process of being published, he can state that the writer must feel the need to communicate, to show his/her work, to let people know about it. He/she should also be aware that writings may be rejected; therefore, he/she should be mentally prepared to modify it and not to take the rejection as personal. The writer may be persuaded to modify the work and to improve it. When the writer can improve the work – after the suggestions are accepted and introduced into the piece of work – he/she will grow as a writer. He/she should be tenacious and believe in him/herself. Even in extreme cases of full rejection, he/she should never repent having written the document. Sometimes, defeats can be bridges to a victory. In the author's personal case, when his first dissertation was ruthlessly and inconsistently criticized some forty years ago in Cuba, his opponents' criticism helped him improve the quality of his dissertation and he finished his defense with flying colors in the former Soviet Union. Parents may play an important role in fostering – in their children – the tenacity to start and finish undertakings, to respect themselves, to love for their work, to accept constructive criticism and – if it is necessary – to start all over again.

- Inborn pedagogic talent. There are professors or teachers who can inspire students with high quality classes that encourage them to be better pupils and to improve their skills in performing their future profession. The truly inborn professor feels the need to deliver knowledge in the best possible way to orient the student to study for learning, and not just for passing grades. If the student is ready to study the lesson before it is delivered, if the student is ready to actively participate in the classroom, and if the student is ready to review notes and study again shortly after class is done, he/she would be in an excellent position to deeply understand the class. The professor's preparation for each class is an indispensable condition for achieving a good class. Memory may fail, but previous preparation should reduce the probability of forgetting some words, if they are closely related to the content of the class. The professor should strive to have a close relationship with the subject matter he/she is explaining to the students. He/she will therefore have more possibilities to go beyond the textbook, and to offer some personal contributions. Since the inborn professor should be up to date with the subject matter he/she is teaching, the docent should foster students' reasoning (instead of memorization skills). Students should be prepared to apply their theoretical knowledge to professional practice, which really coincides completely with the theory of the subject matter. From a theoretical standpoint, most components should be identifiable in the practice of the profession in journals, newspapers, peer reviewed documents or other professional publications. The student should learn, not only from textbooks and published papers, but also from current events taking place in his/her future professional field. He should not expect a particular theoretical example from class to take place in real life in an identical way. Being a professor of economics himself, the author is aware of the validity of the assumption "all other things constant". This assumption is important, because it would be very difficult to understand a law if all components of reality were included in the explanation. Therefore, the student should get deeper into the theoretical background or theoretical basis for practical reality. Consequently he/she will be able to solve real – related to the theory – problems. There will be additional components to the problem that cannot be explained in class. The talented inborn professor should grow in the student and reiterate the need to study for learning. He/she should Introduce the reality of the profession, so the student will be more prepared to understand, focus on, and solve the concrete problems of his/her specialization.

* The inborn professor should be trained in assimilating new subject matters into his own, going the extra mile, thinking outside the box, with possible cooperation from peers or colleagues. As a matter of fact, this professor may become a creator or innovator in the application of the theory taught in university classrooms. It is widely known for many professors or even teachers that – whenever somebody needs to learn something – it would help him or her to teach a class on the topic. When something needs further explanation, the best and

deepest way to do it is to explain it to a student. The pressure of having to teach something to somebody is very often the reason to undertake the adventure of adding knowledge to a profession or even to more general human relations.

- The author states that he does have vocation for teaching because since he was a young man, he became a monitor to his college mates in math, economy, and history, by being selected as pre-graduate instructor of Linear Algebra under the pressure of one week notice without having received previous pedagogical training, and by being recipient of important awards in Cuban, Mexican and American universities.

- Talent or gift of attitude. Tenacity to reach goals. Since the author was a young man – and in the natural process of getting older – whenever he hears news about somebody achieving outstanding results, tenacity is always mentioned as an important reason for the success. Tenacity is indispensable for training the brain and the body, for fostering the will to succeed. Whenever we talk about a scientific discovery, an athlete breaking records, an outstanding artist or singer who has been able to stand out as a singer, an actor, a composer, an orchestra leader, or a musical director the word "tenacity" is reiteratively mentioned. Delving into the root of tenacity's importance, one can learn about the courage and the iron will needed to repeat an experiment until he/she reaches a minimum level of perfection, to fall and to stand up again, to go to extremes of tiredness and to start all over again. Repetition is necessary because it is rare to achieve something extraordinary in a single try. To approve a medicine in the health industry many scientists or specialists must invest years into experimentation involving persons – or sometimes even animals – of different ages and sexes, in several seasons and countries. For a singer to reach fame, he/she must practice reiteratively, to improve his/her singing. A singer must learn to accept low paying jobs at the beginning until he/she acquires prestige, must learn to show his/her talent in different stages, theaters, countries, must learn to be healthy, and, finally, must learn to meet all the requirements stated under different circumstances.

Deeply meditating on the common factors in all successful individuals one can see the following:

1) A successful individual must have the talent of tenacity to reach the goal.
2) He/she must be completely committed to the objective he/she is pursuing.
3) The systematic repetition of attempts is indispensable while working towards the goal.
4) These exercises are conceived to be long range, not short or intermediate.
5) There must exist the conviction – or the very strong ineluctable desire and need – to reach the goal.

Here is a personal example. The author really and badly needed to hold a PhD degree. This was his personal goal as a scholar. He had to overcome scientific, political, and social obstacles. He was subject to four pre-defenses in two countries, to a write dissertation in Spanish, English and Russian. He was required to take four graduate exams in which he had to demonstrate mastery of one language, philosophy, specialty in a subject matter, and economics. He passed with flying colors, two languages, two specialties in a subject matter, philosophy, and economics. But he succeeded only with the research experience acquired during ten years in Great Britain, Cuba, and Ukraine. He *was* tenacious and needed to hold a PhD, which would help him succeed in life, even beyond his expectations.

- Talent for learning foreign languages

Some people are lucky enough to be the descendant of parents who speak different native languages, or to be part of a family, in which some members can express themselves in more than one language. There are unfavorable political, social, or economic situations in which individuals are forced to travel abroad – scarcity of employment, dangerous situations such as revolutions, proliferation of gangs, drug addicts, and so on. The four freedoms – or the key principles at the heart of the European Union – are free movement of goods, services, people, and capital among all countries. Therefore, all individuals experience a deep and justified need to talk, read, and write in more than one language. Europe is composed of many countries in a limited geographical space. It is possible to drive a car – through countries speaking different languages like – Poland, the Czech Republic, and Austria – in less than twenty-four hours. The author would like to emphasize the word "need" as one of the main causes of linguistic multiculturalism during several centuries. Great Britain was one of the most economically powerful countries of the world, conquering and establishing colonies in several continents. Since it was the metropolis of many countries speaking different languages, it needed to introduce and to extend the use of the English language in its colonies. Therefore, it was very unlikely – except the members of the diplomatic sphere – to find inhabitants of England, Scotland or Ireland speaking more than one language. The linguistic need fell to the colonies that needed to speak English to relate economically, politically, and socially with the metropolis. At the end of World War II, the United States substituted Great Britain as the most powerful country in the world; consequently, it is not surprising to learn that very few Americans speak more than one language. In 1958, the author had the opportunity to go from Cuba to the US as a tourist. He already knew English, and it was hard for him to find individuals speaking Spanish. But in 1996, when he arrived in the US again, he was surprised to find many Spanish speaking people in Chicago, and anywhere else he went. The globalization process is a strong reason for this sort of increasing bilingualism in the US, especially as of 1993 – when the NAFTA Treaty was signed by Mexico, Canada, and the United States. The Spanish language is now present as an option in many business and commercial institutions, including newspapers and TV stations.

Many individual cases can be cited, such as an opera Singer learning Italian, or a Cuban student or professor learning Russian, especially in the times of the former Soviet Union. Now it is possible to find a businessman learning Mandarin. It is possible to find exceptional individuals who feel the need to learn a foreign language only because he/she enjoys it. It should be borne in mind that to master a foreign language, it is imperative to practice it orally, in writing, and listening systematically during many years. It is necessary to keep it alive in the brain.

A sentence from https://www.fluentin3months.com/reading-writing-speaking-and-listening, which is very relevant to this topic of language learning, says: "Writing; Listening; Speaking. The skills work in pairs. When you are reading or listening, you are consuming a language. However, when you are writing or speaking, your area is producing a language. Once you have mastered these skills, you can safely say that you are fluent in that language."

The native language is less demanding than the foreign one because the former is embodied in the brain. In the author's opinion, the native language is preferred even by most polyglots because an individual can express himself in the mother language using the most adequate words to express the deeper feelings of a human being.

The author had a talent for learning foreign languages because he has lived for many years in countries where different languages are spoken. Therefore, he is able to fluently speak Spanish, English and Russian. He was blessed to acquire a solid Spanish grammar in grade school and in secondary education. Thanks to this skill it wasn't hard for him to learn Russian because of the prevalence of the cases – in subjects and direct and indirect objects – which require that all words be written and pronounced with different endings. Italian wasn't that hard because it is relatively like Spanish. Surprisingly enough, the author did not have an accent in Italian, but he does have it in English and Russian. His main reason for studying Italian was that his first boss was Italo-American, and he was the secretary. He has visited Italy only as a tourist on three occasions. He learned French because – before doing his master's degree in Scotland – he was originally to be sent to France for this purpose. He has visited Paris as a tourist on three occasions.

It is his personal conclusion that the main reason to study and be fluent in a foreign language is to speak, to write or to listen to it… and it is indispensable to practice it systematically.

- Talent or virtue for traveling around the world due to academic or personal reasons.

Among highly educated people – or in individuals who attended and finished college degrees – it is not unusual to find curiosity about visiting or temporarily living in foreign countries, or dreams of celebrating special occasions like marriages, birthdays, anniversaries in foreign countries. It gives people like this satisfaction to get one's feet in famous world cities like Paris, London, Madrid, Rio de Janeiro, Buenos Aires, New York, Chicago, Miami, Berlin, Warsaw, etc. Not everybody has the possibility of traveling around the world, and not everyone can learn the language of the country he/she is about to visit.

If one analyzes the possibility of traveling abroad for a person born in Cuba – as a direct result of economic and political restrictions imposed in this country after 1959 – even within the context of developing countries with limited access to foreign currency, one will soon conclude that it is very difficult for a Cuban to be a traveler of the world. To travel abroad, one faces two big obstacles, one of them is that it is not cheap to travel, especially after the triumph of the revolution in 1959. The second most important one is the inflexibility exerted by the government in the process of "allowing" citizens to leave the country by imposing on them the need to be approved or denied in consideration of his/her rejection or approval of the Communist Party's power over the people. If the country of origin were not an island, surrounded by the Gulf of Mexico and the Caribbean Sea, it would have been easier for Cubans to travel abroad. Many of its citizens wouldn't have needed to use a raft across the sea and to risk – and frequently lose – their lives. The Cuban diaspora is dispersed around the world although most of its members reside in the United States of America. This is a direct result of the Communist revolution doing away with the people's freedom to voluntarily choose their leaders. The Cuban people were also forced to live miserably without any hope of change, and they are subject to a very strong political repression. The main reason the Cuban diaspora traveled abroad was the fact that it was impossible or unbearable for them to live in absolute mediocrity with a lack of freedom being widespread and predominating in Cuba. The desire to know the world was not one of the government's priorities.

The material possibility of enjoying world traveling is largely concentrated to North Americans, West Europeans, Japanese and Chinese. Another indispensable condition is to possess enough financial resources in a foreign currency. It might happen, though, that even wealthy citizens of the above nationalities don't feel motivated to travel in planes, cruises, trains or sometimes in vehicles.

Curiously enough, traveling abroad sometimes elicits a nostalgic desire in travelers to return to their country of origin because they miss the places where they used to live comfortably – familiar with the different idiosyncrasies and customs they are used to enjoying. The best combination of traveling and being at home is leaving the country for days, weeks or months, returning, and going abroad again. The author considers this combination to be a part of an individual's right of choice, so inherent to the American way of life.

The combination of a vocation for travel, the possession of necessary financial resources, the flexibility of having paid vacations, and the need to experience – first hand – cities, civilizations, and countries of special connotations and importance normally make up the set of components frequently found in the travelers of the world.

The author has this talent for travel because of the way his life took place in Cuba. He had some privileges, like: (1). Traveling – when he was seventeen years old – as a tourist to America just six months before 1959 using his own resources and the favorable conditions created by my first boss at *El Mundo* newspaper in Havana and inspired by his mother's original recommendation that he interrupted his pre-college studies to learn English, (2). Traveling to

Scotland – when he was thirty years old – for a master's degree after finishing his baccalaureate studies. Before completing his baccalaureate career, he was obliged to be a docent in Operational Research. The scholarship was specifically based on his specialization as a young professor, and that was the only faculty able to speak English in a scholarly environment, (3). Traveling to the Soviet Union – from 1981 to 1990 when he was in his forties – to receive his PhD and doctorate after his extensive experience as a scholar, the publication of his books, and his previous preparation in the Russian language. He wrote and defended two dissertations in Russian, (4). Traveling to Mexico for three years – when he was in his early fifties – as a professor and leader of a research team made of instructors and students in environmental economics. He was the only doctor in economics specialized in the subject matter, (5). Traveling to the University of Chicago –while he was teaching in Mexico – financed by an American Foundation because he was the only faculty specialized in environmental economics, (6). Traveling to the United States as a scholar and being granted the political asylum status when he was 55; and finally, after becoming an American resident and citizen (7) Traveling from Chicago to around the world. Although he never had a credit card or any idea about credit ratings before coming to the US, he had enough education and had control over his emotions, a tenacity in achieving goals and an iron will to become a financially responsible American with an excellent credit rating. During Gladys' last eleven years, she accompanied the author in visiting many foreign countries. He has been a traveler of the world for the last sixteen years.

His talent for traveling around the world – despite being born in Cuba –was possible because of his academic achievements, his tenacity in reaching goals, and his financial responsibility. He paid off his mortgage in ten years and had a reverse mortgage, and used the efficient transportation in Chicago –which rendered inconvenient the possession of a car – chose a home close to his work places, made wise investments in insurance policies and hasn't had a single cent of debt since his arrival in this great country in 1996. Taking care of his health through a diet based on fruits, vegetables, fish, chicken, and occasionally beef, systematic physical exercising at home, and being a nonsmoker, and non-drinker. It is also important to underline his positive reaction to the grief of losing the woman in his life. He gives credit to his extraordinary wife for many of his achievements. He is a happy man thanks to her although she died in his arms on October 5, 2015. Death could not separate them!

- Talent for singing

Singing might be defined as a pleasant way to be happy. It is possible to sing either efficiently or deficiently simply with the purpose of killing idle time. According to the opinion of several physicians, the author has learned that singing helps him to have a positive attitude and to beat – or at least reduce – stress, which is one of his main enemies. Anybody can sing either with talent or without it. Normally the inborn singers find themselves among the people who enjoy feeling the vibration of their voices and love to transmit happiness to those around them.

There are individuals who were born with good, pleasant, and powerful voices that range from the ranges of sopranos, tenors, baritone, mezzo-soprano, as well as good voices that correspond to lighter types of popular or even dancing songs. There are singers whose performance environment is their home or their intimate friends. They may be afraid to show their vocal capacities in public. To sing well depends on an individual's natural singing conditions, which can be improved by taking singing lessons from recognized specialist teachers. There are some singers – like the author of this book – who discover their singing powers in a coincidental, involuntary, or unexpected way. The singer may receive a surprise when he receives congratulations or comments of approval while he asks himself: "Who is singing here? I do not recognize that voice".

In my case, the author always loved singing since he was a boy. Some of his English teachers were Frank Sinatra, Nat King Cole, and the Platters, who simultaneously taught him vocabulary and expressions like "falling in love", which confused him the first time he heard it. During the mass offered to honor Gladys' extraordinary life, the author had the opportunity to sing in public. At the end of the mass, he dedicated his song to Gladys. He sang an a cappella the Italian song that he had sung to her during their initial rendezvous when they were young. Suddenly, the author did not recognize the powerful voice that echoed in the church like thunder. He was mesmerized and further surprised to receive very positive comments from his friends. On October 16th, 2015, Antonio, the public singer, was born.

There are singers who only sing in private groups of friends. They don't feel prepared to sing in front of unknown people, who might impolitely criticize them. On the other end of the range of singer spectrum, there are individuals who enjoy singing to unknown groups of individuals just for the fun of bringing joy and entertainment to multitudes, whether where the performance is delivered in a theater, in a TV program, or in front of judges in a competition.

The inborn singer enjoys his art, feels the vibration of his voice when it transits or flows when it is accompanied by a piano, or an orchestra. He/she knows how to identify him/herself with the music and enjoys recognizing and adhering to a good tone. The inborn singer recognizes the moments to rise or to reduce the voice, and when or for how long to extend the end of the song. The best non-economic way to pay homage to a singer is by clapping hands or rounds of applause coming from fans standing up and shouting "bravo".

He/she may be inborn or created under the influence of external conditions.

<u>Talent for resisting and reducing the grief of losing a loved one</u>

Death is the irreversible cessation of life. It is that is always feared by those familiar with the deceased person. Analyzing the ninth chapter of *Gladys, My Unforgettable Love*, and meditating about her extraordinary and brave behavior – reaching and spreading empathy all over around her – the author has been able to deduce and to generalize some conditions for reducing grief and instilling hope and good humor in a person who is witnessing the progressive deterioration of a deeply loved person.

Important assumption. To implement Gladys' masterful performance in the way she managed the situation of her imminent death, it is necessary to know in advance that the unfortunate is likely to happen within within months or weeks. In other words, her performance is not applicable when death is either unforeseeable, or unexpectedly violent, such as in the case of a fatal accident.

According to the Cambridge English dictionary's definition of empathy, it is one person's ability to understand and share somebody else's feelings. In a common English conversation, we say "to walk a mile in somebody else's shoes".

To be empathic is not an easy task. Not everybody can – or feels the need to – be empathic. It is possible to be empathic with some people – especially if the person is one of your friends or loved ones – but not with everyone. In the just mentioned unlikely case the empathic person is ready to help another individual although he/she might be an enemy, who is against your beliefs or personal interests.

In other words, the empathic person must be a good person from a human point of view, ready to help anybody in need. Gladys was like the described person with almost everybody she met, and the author was the man whom she wanted to improve despite sometimes going against his conscious will. The author refers the reader to the concept of "pure diamond" mentioned in *Gladys, My Unforgettable Love*, which clearly refers to an empathic behavior.

For a year and a half, Gladys was seriously ill and constantly struggled to breathe, having to use a portable oxygen device. She never complained about her health problems and never cried. She knew very well and just by looking in my eyes, she could observe that the author was suffering to see how she was slowly dying. During times he couldn't voluntarily hold back his tears. She started to make fun of him to the point of scolding him, saying that he did not have the right to cry because he had made her a happy woman during their forty years together. All the time she felt his support, his protective strength, his love, and commitment to her. She always could feel his love and he had nothing to be regretful or remorseful over. When the nurses started extracting blood from her thin veins, he couldn't look at the scene because she was suffering intensely, but she was able – even under those painful circumstances – to smile and encourage the nurses. The author was totally dedicated to thinking about how to help her, how to reduce her pain, how to make her my love with words and actions, how to constantly repeat close to her ears "how much I loved and admired her". He was in a constant process of being empathetic. On her behalf, he ran the extra mile, and several times went out of his way to be close to her – regardless of the circumstances he was going through. He had never ever been so committed to anybody else's happiness. To make her happy if she was alive was the main purpose of his life. He had the confirmation that he had become an empathic human being when – shortly before passing away – she told him that he had become a pure diamond. In conclusion, Gladys died with the peace of mind knowing that her man was not going to suffer, that he would continue being happy paying homage to her. He felt at peace thinking about ways to pay homage to her extraordinary sacrifice and love. He made up his mind to spread the word about her exceptionalism, and – being a writer – he felt the need to write the book *Gladys, My Unforgettable Love*, which has become his concrete way to show empathy to all his readers. He sincerely wishes that this noble mutual feeling be transmitted to all couples who feel the forthcoming unfortunate event of losing one member. To follow her example is a sure way of reducing the grief and recovering the happiness of being alive.

In conclusion, the "recipe" that the author can recommend to any couples trying to recover happiness is empathy. When one of the members of the couple is empathetic toward the other, he/she will create a mutual influx of reciprocal empathy and love. Let us now analyze the role of each member.

The role of the survivor is to try to think about the dying member all the time. Concentrate your attention in the happy moments you shared with him/her and support that person with all your heart. Express your love with words and – whenever possible – with actions. There is not much time left to do so; consequently, repeat the procedure as much as possible. The harder you try, the more you can put yourself in her/his shoes. The other person will feel that you want to make her/him feel happy, and – this is very important – the other person will feel the conviction you have that sickness had not diminished your love for him/her. Surprise her/him with unannounced small gifts. When the surviving member takes these actions to pleasantly surprise the dying member, his/her behavior clearly shows that you are thinking about him/her all the time even when you cannot physically be together. Gladys experienced such a delight whenever I gave her even one flower, especially if she was not expecting it. You will show your partner that your love for him/her is so strong that it is able to remind you of moments that – before the sickness invaded your lives – you could both enjoy. True love is the one that brings your souls together even when the sickness does not allow sexual relations. This is the love that defeats death. Your love will not cease with the physical disappearance of one member of the couple.

The role of the dying person is to resist pain as much as possible, trying to think of ways to reduce the other member's psychological distress. Try to talk about the best moments of your togetherness. That will give the other person the consolation of knowing that you brought bliss to her/his life, that you are each other's mutual rock, that he/she was the only owner of your love. If one grows in love, one will most likely harvest love, but this is a type of love especially conceived as the contact of the souls and the support of hugs, kisses, caresses, tender gazes, and romantic looks. These mutual, respectful, and lovely interactions foster the growth of empathetic feelings that allow the internal communication between the two members. The dying member feels more accompanied, while the survivor feels better, more peaceful, and more prepared for the definitive moment. His/her conscience will be more peaceful and can start the preparation process for recovering happiness.

Food for thought
The readers are recommended to analyze themselves as far as their talents are concerned. Has the reading of this

chapter helped them to identify which are their talents; and whether they are being used either for their benefit or for somebody else's?

Let us now analyze each one of my loves individually.

Chapter IV

Its contents deal with the way in which the talents are related to those of the two women who had considerably influenced the performance of the author's life, his mother and his second wife. Firstly, each person individually; secondly, in pairs along with the author… in other words, as mother-son, husband-wife; and finally, integrated in a trio.

4.1 My First Love: My Mother (Siria Pita Allende)

"When you are a mother, you are never alone in your thoughts. A mother always must think twice, once for herself and once for her child."

Sophia Loren

"My mother's love has always been a sustaining force for our family, and one of my greatest joys is seeing her integrity, her compassion, her intelligence reflected in my daughters."

Michelle Obama

"Youth fades; love droops; the leaves of friendship fall; a mother's secret hope outlives them all."

Oliver Wendell Homes

The author's mother was an exceptional woman, who loved life, work and being actively useful. She was a very energetic person, as can be deducted from the wide range of her diverse activities. She was a nice person, completely dedicated to her home, and to her four children. From her, he inherited quite a few of his talents. Let's analyze from which of them, she experienced a more noticeable development.

Siria Pita's most outstanding merit is that despite being illiterate – because she was born into a poor family whose income did not allow her to attend school – she felt an insatiable need to learn, and to understand the world around her. She loved to study, to grow in her children a passion for studying, for reading, and demanding her offspring study in libraries during school vacations. She frequently visited our school, constantly urged us to do our homework – although she couldn't answer any of the questions related to the courses her children were taking. When she was 51 years old, she started learning how to read and write. By the time she had completed her 82nd birthday – she was finished with pre-college education. She became an example to everybody, to members and nonmembers of the family alike. She encouraged young people not to waste time and to continue their education. Siria enjoyed learning and sharing her knowledge with the family. Her eyes glittered when she understood elementary topics like the fact that the earth was round and that the moon was a satellite of the

Earth, constantly spinning around our planet. For her to learn was a fantastic experience! She always tried to speak as correctly as possible, and I never heard an incorrectly pronounced word from her!

Her second most outstanding merit was her tenacity in undertaking any type of work assigned to her. She wanted to fulfill all her goals which –sometimes – she assigned to herself. She usually combined tenacity with punctuality. As a matter of fact, she could not be unpunctual because she was very tenacious and organized in tackling any task assigned to her. Her tenacity was present, not only in the chores at home, but also in systematic physical training on a rustic stationary bike located in the smallest room of the house. She always had to finish whatever she started. On turning 68 years old, she persuaded her husband to allow her to become an employee in a nearby children's clothes workshop. Despite being the eldest worker, she broke all time norms for each type of cloth and was chosen as cutting-edge manual sewer. She was awarded with one – week of paid vacation at a nearby beach. She went on her own because my father did not have the necessary energy to accompany her.

During the author's last stay in the former Soviet Union – the same day he was to defend his dissertation, and without previous notice – she visited him dorm in Kiev. When the author *learned* of his mother's arrival at the dorm, he could hardly believe his eyes. She was admired by her younger friends because she participated in each one of her tour groups, activities, never got tired and encouraged the younger travelers to imitate her.

She always supported him in the different studies he undertook. When he turned fourteen years old, he had finished secondary education and was getting ready to enter pre-college. She approached him and asked him to start studying English instead. The unusual change in his studies was because his family needed him to financially contribute to maintain our home as soon as possible. Knowing English would allow him to start working as a bilingual secretary without having to wait for his graduation from a university. This was his first big educational challenge as a student because he only had rudimentary knowledge of the English language – as it was usually taught in grade school in Cuba. To study as a full-time student would require a previous higher level of elementary English and a systematic dedication to the language for at least eight hours per day.

At this point the author mentions a circumstance that shows the impact his mother had on his student life. He was enrolled at the Havana Business Academy, which was widely known for its educational strictness in assigning students to different levels of English based on their level of vocabulary, grammar, reading and writing skills. He had to do a vocabulary exam. His level of preparation was so low that he had to guess on multiple choice quizzes. He ignored most of the words, but he had a sort of guessing feeling that indicated to him which answers were right. As a result, he was placed in a level that was higher than the one he was really at. The academy principal was so surprised by his grade on the exam that she offered to his mother – who accompanied him in this adventure – the possibility of placing him in a lower level if he felt that level six was too high for him. The higher the initial level, the sooner he would finish his studies and that was in line with his mother's objectives. Therefore, she told the principal that she trusted in his academic capacity and intelligence. During the first two weeks the pressure was enormous on his brain – of course he did not know, then, that he would be facing harder challenges soon, and that this effort would prepare him – but he never gave up. Whenever he consulted his mother's opinion – when he resisted standing up after a fall – or when he felt overwhelmed by the amount of difficult tasks he had undertaken, her answer was always, "Listen, my son, always prepare your mind to go ahead, never backwards. You always must demand extra effort from yourself to grow and to succeed. Do not ever, ever, give up." As a result, he never felt defeated, and always finished whatever he had started. What a way to positively influence his student life and performance!

Because of his mother's unusually original idea that he study the English language before starting high school, he was able to prepare himself to become a young professor in Linear Algebra and Linear Programming because all the textbooks were written in English. He chose to pursue a master's in Operational Research in Scotland, because he was the only English-speaking professor in his department at the College of Economics of the University of Havana. He was chosen in an exchange of scholars between the University of Chicago and the University of Havana – while he was working in Mexico. On top of that, he was able to attain the zenith of his higher education career with his second doctorate in the former Soviet Union, which was validated in America. Eventually this allowed him to become a faculty member at DePaul University, the largest Catholic university in the United States.

In evaluating his mother's influence on his life, he should recognize that his mother also had negative human weaknesses. He was the preferred child, who had fulfilled all her aspirations as a student, the first one to enter and to finish college, and the only one who finished his studies as a professor. He was the spoiled one at home, much more than any of his siblings, and she created divisions between them. When he was a child, he was constantly kissing her in a more systematic and frequent way than any of her other children. Simultaneously she should also recognize that he was kind hearted, complacent with ladies, somewhat conceited by handsomeness and he found acceptance among young ladies.

After dating some lovers – all of whom were older women – he married at the young age of twenty-two. He became a father in his early and middle twenties. He was not loyal to his first wife, specifically during his time in Scotland, where a Scottish lady – Lorna – unleashed his male potency. He fell deeply in love with her. On his return to Cuba, he became totally aware that his wife was not able to make her happy. There were some intellectual vacuums between them that interfered with their mutual understanding and happiness. Two years after his return from Scotland, he received the first rented apartment of his life as a prize – granted by the then president of the University of Havana – for being the first master's in science in the College of Economics. Since his wife was living with his children in his father's home, until he could find a home for them, it would be very difficult for him to get divorced. Therefore, one year after living in the new home, he gave them the apartment and started a new life as a divorced man. Following his father's example as a committed father, he kept his fatherhood at a good level. He needed his children to understand that the divorce was not from them, and that they could always count on their father. Despite sleeping in different homes for seven years, he dedicated two or three hours most Saturdays to study with them during their time in primary and secondary schools. They followed the same student vocation and performance as he did, enrolling and finishing college. Coincidentally both finished their baccalaureate degrees at approximately the same time as he defended his second dissertation in the same foreign country – the Soviet Union. One of the dearest and warmest Father's Day that he remembers took place in Kiev in 1987. His son and his daughter – who were studying in Moscow and Lvov respectively – stayed with him for three days in Kiev in his own room. Those three days they were singing together – remembering the times when they were children and would try to guess the title of the song. The author speaks five languages; his son speaks three and his daughter speaks two languages. The three of them felt the need to learn foreign languages.

As a divorced and lady's man, he continued desperately looking for his Cuban Lorna for five years after his return from Scotland. It was then that he met Gladys – who found her happiness with him – without ever imagining that she would be able to transform him into a much better human being. How could she, or he, imagine that the child so spoiled by Siria Pita would become an empathic man? Gladys' love for him was so deep and true that she assumed the difficult task of transforming the gentleman – who despite being good, "deep down" – was like a tarnished diamond, full of deficiencies, which she would attempt to eliminate. She could do it because she had some of his mother's talents, besides some others that only a wife could possess. Both intertwined their virtues and placed them in the author of this book. It was like a substitution race when one lady runner gives the baton to the other, and the victory is for them both. The goal was to make him a better human being. Now, let us analyze Gladys' talents which she shared with him until dying in his arms after forty years, six months and one day of shared happiness and absolute spiritual and material unity. Their love was not separated by her death, rather it is still alive taking care of the transformed diamond.

In the beginning of this book, the author enumerated the seven talents that the Lord has given to him. Some of them were studied in the case of his mother. Now it is time to look at his wife – Gladys Núñez Díaz, whose name was changed to Gladys Morales when they arrived in the United States. While in his mother's case her gifts are found in the educational dimension, in the determination of fulfilling good objectives, and in the tenacity and resilience to successfully finish undertakings of different nature, in Gladys' case there is a virtue or talent that 'prominently' – and in a splendorous, gorgeous, magnificent fashion – stands out with a truly amazing strength while simultaneously being deeply human. He is referring to the empathy she manifested in the way she faced death and trained the man in her life in such a way that he never suffered after her physical disappearance.

4.2 My Second Love: My Wife (Gladys)

"A virtuous woman is not moved by big names and flamboyance, but only men of profound wisdom and integrity move her."

Michael Bassey Johnson

"A woman, who knows how to be on her knees, can overcome any battle with ease."

Gift Gugu Mona, *Woman of Virtue: Power-Filled Quotes for a Powerful Woman*

Gladys establishes an impressive precedent of empathy because hers was a transcendental alleviation in human suffering. Going back to his mother's talents, they helped herself, the closest members of her family and individuals who met and respected her – in the first place her beloved youngest son, who is the most benefited because he was the one in closest contact with her. He assimilated – and introduced into his personality and performance – the tenacity, the desire to live and to be useful, to overcome difficulties, to attain educational and scientific relevance, as well as preference and passion for traveling around the world.

Gladys transcends beyond her own life. She died in moments of extreme happiness with the man in her life, silently bearing frequent pains, having trouble breathing, and sleeping very few hours per day. Under these circumstances she was more concerned about her man's state of mind than her own because he was the one who would suffer the most because of her physical disappearance. Although she was a very smart and analytic woman, her humility did not allow her to catch a glimpse of her example of stoicism, selflessness, and empathy which could be passed on to somebody else going through similar circumstances. Her spontaneous simplicity – and even naivety – was an obstacle that obstructed Gladys from being aware of her own greatness, although it was easy for her to notice the greatness in others. How could she imagine that her laudable attitude and performance – her protection of her lover from the suffering of being alone in the same house where they lived together for more than forty years – could be written in a book and be read by couples going through similar painful circumstances by providing them consolation and energy to go on with their lives? This much needed support is transmitted, not only to the survivor, but also to the one near death because the latter may wait for the event in peace of mind knowing that her/his partner is being prepared to deal with grief.

Empathy – which was deeply rooted in the author's lover's personality – was the basis of her performance. Since Gladys was able to put herself in somebody else's shoes, she could sense and even feel the effect that her words would have on the recipients of her message.

It is true that Gladys always had an empathic attitude, although there were crucial moments in which this supreme feeling invaded her and induced an incredible emergence and abundance of kindness. For the woman in his life one of these situations took place from July 1995 and the summer of 1996 during their first stay in a Chicago hostel while they were waiting to receive asylum status.

During this period, Gladys courageously faced our physical separation due to the unfair retention of the author's passport by the Cuban government – always prioritizing the situation of the couple over her own. She had the courage to avoid being unfairly deported from Mexico due to a request from the Cuban consulate in Merida. She simultaneously continued working as a professor in a Mexican university, establishing close contact with the leaders of the Mexican Institute of Technology keeping them aware of his situation and receiving feedback from them to facilitate his rescue from Cuba from, maintaining weekly epistolary communication through passengers flying between Merida and Havana. She intensely studied English during our first year in the US, and even overcame the violence in Humboldt Park, Chicago. During these difficult times, she kept a permanent smile on her face. Her supportive and encouraging words were always present between them. She was constantly thinking about how to reduce the tension he was going through. She never cried, never complained about anything, she was always optimistic. In those crucial periods of our lives, he was engrossed in the urgent issues of political asylum, and he couldn't appreciate the human greatness of the woman moving around him. He hasn't yet realized that he was her rock, and that she was his. Even though he was the only guilty person whose unfortunate visit to Cuba in July 1995 went against her will and warning advice, she never reproached him for not listening to her. She was able to foretell that some terrible event would happen during his visit to the country where he was going to visit his sick and ailing mother. Unconsciously, he had obliged her to go though some thorny issues in which they both suffered due to his mistake.

During their forty years of togetherness, she always kept an empathetic and understanding attitude.

While understanding that the majority of studied talents or gifts can be attained by some people – although very few are able to have and apply them into their performances – the gift of empathy can be transmitted to other individuals' consciences and performances. It is necessary that the recipient of this talent have deep conditions of solidarity and commitment towards humanity. He/she must be kind, charitable, mentally prepared to be a better person, and able to make sacrifices – at least partially – for other human beings. By writing, talking about and promoting this book, the author is formally assuming the responsibility of transmitting her example to the readers. The task is hard to undertake. The reader should make up his/her mind about the beneficial feeling of empathy. The author leaves the decision to the reader to feel whether life is more worth living with empathy. It may also happen that – often – happiness will be at his/her disposal more frequently.

Besides being empathic, the woman in his life had the talent of writing and reading. Since she was a little girl, studying in grade school in the country of the Havana province, she excelled above her classmates in her intelligence, her good behavior and capacity for learning. Although she never could publish a book, she wrote pedagogical monographs for studying Spanish, which were created for the specific conditions of Hispanic immigrants preparing for college. It was satisfying for her to write for the poor, the humble immigrants arriving in this country without any knowledge of English. When Gladys arrived in Chicago in 1996, she did not know how to speak, write or read in English. Nonetheless, during her first two years – by means of a huge and tenacious commitment – she found ways to acceptably express herself in the foreign language. Since she was used to expressing herself in complex sentences, and had a deep knowledge of Spanish grammar, she couldn't content herself by using simple sentences in English. She started to teach business in Spanish at St. Augustine College in Chicago, but after a couple of years, she could do it in English. She contributed to training Hispanic students as small businessmen and women. Although she had never received any course related to pedagogy, her systematic empathic behavior made it easy for her to get the message across to her students, to be aware of their educational difficulties, and to help them overcome them. She was a respected and beloved teacher for her students at St. Augustine College.

Tenacity was always present in her as a student, as a worker, and as a leader in her professional work as accountant in governmental institutions in Cuba, such as the construction industry. Nonetheless there were two aspects of her personality in which – unfortunately – she could not have a tenacious performance. In her initial years as a worker, she was encouraged to smoke by a friend of hers. She also used to practice – especially in her teens or early twenties – physical exercises, but after her first marriage, she fell out of practice. During some decades she unsuccessfully tried to stop smoking and start going back to the gym, but there was always a reason she couldn't materialize her intentions. Since the author had never smoked in his life, and – on top of that – he enjoyed exercising even under difficult circumstances, he could not put himself in her shoes and consistently and unsuccessfully criticized her two failures. The reader of *Gladys, My Unforgettable Love*, may remember that the author mentioned in its prologue how it was that she finally – after her sickness had advanced to a point of no return – stopped smoking. The author did not criticize her in a persuasive way. For her, smelling the nicotine aroma on her made him uncomfortable. It was almost impossible for him not to avoid starting arguments which – at the end of the day – were ineffective.

As far as the talent of learning foreign language is concerned, the reader already knows that Gladys became bilingual shortly after arriving in the US Despite learning a new language in her late forties – she could read, write, and speak correctly in both English and Spanish.

The author helped her in becoming an international traveler. At the end of 2009 and beginning of 2010 both of them had to be hospitalized because of blocked arteries. They both received prosthesis and stents without needing to have open-heart operations. These simultaneous events led us to think about the shortness of life and the need to enjoy it as much as they could. When they became American citizens in 2004, it was easier for them to travel around the world. Together they visited Spain, England, France, Italy, Germany, Poland, Slovakia, the Czech Republic, Austria, Dubai, and they took ocean cruises in the Caribbean Sea, to Alaska, the Mediterranean and North seas. In their last year together, they spent time remembering those unforgettable experiences and were happy to have made the decision to travel around the world. They always traveled in a way in which their finances would not be compromised. They always were inclined to accept the least expensive options. The facts that they didn't have a car – their home in Chicago is geographically close to downtown and to the lake which made it unnecessary to spend a lot of money for parking – the fact that they worked hard, that they paid their mortgage off in ten years and that they were covered by a reverse mortgage, the fact that they never spent more than they had in their savings accounts in one credit card cycle, that they had excellent credit ratings without paying one cent in interest, and that they had life and health insurances – these allowed them to become travelers of the world.

The front cover of the Spanish version of *Gladys, My Unforgettable Love* was taken from a photo the author took of Gladys during our Alaskan ocean cruise. Its backdrop shows one of the Alaskan glaciers. It is interesting to note that involuntarily – given his limited experience as photographer – the reader can see that the smile on her face is like that of Monalisa from Leonardo da Vinci' famous painting. She seems to be smiling, but not in an open way as if she wanted the audience to meditate on her expression. Her face doesn't express either happiness or sadness, but something suggests a sharpness of thought. Another point of coincidence with Mona Lisa's picture is that she is directly looking at the observer. Whatever position is taken by the observer – from the right or the left, from the bottom or the top of the photo – she is looking directly at him/her.

It was easy to perceive that Gladys is naturally beautiful, with the minimum make-up in her lips and brows. Her face come out showing the black color of her hair, whose dye helped her to conceal the white hairs covering every piece of her head. The author does not know whether he is influenced by how much he loved and continues to love her after her death, but he finds her to be gorgeous, strikingly, ravishingly beautiful. The photo is a legitimate and genuine copy of her.

Now that he had analyzed the talents of his two women, he will do his best to show the inter-relationship between them, as well as their complementarity and convergence in his being.

4.3 The Interaction Between Mother And Son

"A mother's arms are more comforting than anyone else's."

Princess Diana.

"If love is as sweet as a flower, then my mother is that sweet flower of love."

Steve Wonder

"My mother is my root, my foundation. She planted the seed that I base my life on, and that is the belief that the ability to achieve starts in your mind."

Michael Jordan

The members of the Morales-Pita family were the following:

- An excellent, hard-working, strict, and responsible father, whose basic dedication was to maintain his home financially, he was intelligent, and rigorously demanded his offspring be moral, principled, and decent citizens. When he was eight years old, he had to maintain his mother and three sisters taming horses in the Havana province countryside. Therefore, he could never attend school. Although he could not read, he managed to learn some basic mathematical operations. Up to the end of his life, he visited his sisters every day. He oversaw solving all the economic and physical needs of his home. He was married to the author's mother for six decades. Although they never got divorced, he was not loyal to my mother. His infidelity was never forgiven by my mother, who subsequently concentrated her love on her children, especially on the author of this book.

- A very loving mother, who took care of the health and education of her children, although she had individual preferences which negatively impacted her children's unity. Since the author was the youngest child and extremely loving with her, she felt responsible for his relations with the opposite sex. Siria Pita was very demanding with each one of his girlfriends and rejected divorced women who were ten or fifteen years older than him – although they were ideal for him because there was no danger of getting married, and he wanted to learn the basics of manly relations with women. Since he was a young bachelor without a taste of compromise, his mother opposed all his girlfriends and treated all of them without consideration. She insisted – and tried all she could – to marry him to a virgin. When he met the future mother of his children, she took the initiative – without previously consulting him or his father – to precipitate his marriage by giving them the largest room of the family home. She needed to supervise the development of his marriage and to be close to her future grandchildren. So, the author's first marriage took place when he was twenty-two years old, and he became a father when he was twenty-three and again at twenty-seven. As a matter of fact, he was not totally in love with his wife. From the very beginning of their marriage, he noticed differences between them in relation to their mutual educational levels and work experiences. His mother wanted her to study and was ready to help with the children, but his wife did not very much like the idea of continuing her studies. Siria Pita was always talking about being responsible in fulfilling our duties as students and workers with tenacity and punctuality, in whatever task was available to them.

- His brother – ten years older than him – and two intermediate sisters. His brother got married when he was nineteen years old and built his home far away from the family home. Before the revolution, it was possible for newly married couples to rent apartments, so he escaped his initial family home.

The author was ten years old when he left; consequently, he never had any interchange of ideas with him, and he did not feel confident to talk to his father about his relations with women because he never welcomed these types of conversations. Of course, his mother could not advise him, so he had to venture himself to acquire sexual experience on his own with very little family assistance. The communication between the four siblings was very weak and – in general terms – everyone but the author built their family away from home. His two sisters had unfortunate marriages, and so did he. His brother was the only one of them who never got divorced. Having said so, all of them learned how to be good, punctual, and tenacious employees. He was the only one to make a living as a research fellow or professor in higher education institutions. All of them – without having the option to say no – were forced to learn how to play piano. He was the only one who felt passion for singing within the limits of his home and his closest friends.

Siria Pita was responsible for cooking, and taking direct care of their lives, their studies, and their health. She taught them to exercise systematically, to eat healthily and to visit the doctors' offices as soon as they felt somewhat sick, especially at the beginning of their sicknesses. She told them to be tenacious and strongly discouraged procrastination. Nobody ever smoked at home, arrived late to any official or important activity, and everybody was always responsible for his/her duties. His mother made them tenacious in starting and finishing whatever task they undertook.

The author was the number one spoiled child because he was his mother's refuge – especially after the discovery of his father's infidelity – besides being her pride in school due to his high grades. She always defended him regardless of the situation. There is another factor unrelated to his faulty upbringing as a child. He was born in a poor, small wooden house, whose inhabitants were his parents, four children and one grandmother. When he was three months old, his father won the Lottery twice, rationally used his financial resources, and elevated the economic level of their family to the middle class, where he could satisfy his whims as a spoiled child. Their new home turned out to be the prettiest and largest in the neighborhood, with direct participation of his father in planning, conceiving, and building it. The author would not have to attend public schools, and his parents could improve the quality of his education in private institutions.

Summarizing this section of the book, his first love created him in a hardworking, studious, and tenacious lover of reading and writing, with pedagogical talents and noteworthy efforts to raise his educational level. Despite his bad uprising – having reached his adult life and having become the father of two children – he was a nice man "deep down" who felt good helping other people if his personal interests were not negatively affected. This is the man who – after an unfortunate marriage – tenaciously tried to find the woman in his life, who could complete his happiness some years after enjoying a successful romance in Great

Britain. Antonio was mentally prepared to meet that lady who could make a happy man out of him although – to achieve this objective – she would have to be strong enough to love him deeply and to transmit to him her naturally empathetic nature.

4.4 The Interaction Between Husband and Wife

"To love someone deeply gives you strength. Being loved by someone deeply gives you courage."

Chinese Philosopher Lao Tzu

"A successful marriage requires falling in love many times, always with the same person."

Mignon McLoughlin

A miracle took place on February 5, 1975. Over the course of eight unforgettable hours this author's mind was favorably surprised by a beautiful lady who was rejecting his caresses – even though she had told him about her premonition that he would be the man in her life. What he did not know was that this same lady would change his life forever. He felt deeply attracted to the lady who asked for absolute fidelity from a man she had just met. And – on top of that – he had told her that he was used to changing women once he got bored of them. Where did she come from? She told him that she was unhappily married, but her way of thinking was like that of an innocent virgin. Her sincerity became crystal clear to him just by analyzing her beautiful brown eyes, her carefully delicate make-up, combined with a soft feminine voice. She would accept neither lies nor betrayal. Some months after she got divorced from her husband – with whom she was unfortunately married for five years – he came to understand deeply that she was an exceptional human being. She deserved his absolute confidence even from our first rendezvous. Sincerity came out of her eyes, her words, her face, her whole body. The author was enthralled by her!

A lovely romance was born – in which they appeared to be a couple of "young lovers" intertwining hands, hugging strongly, and starting a period of mutual acquaintance in which there were no lies, or infidelities. Every day, on several occasions, they talked over the phone. The moment when they said good-bye was always interrupted or postponed with kisses, with laughter, or with an unexpected event demanding an unwanted farewell. But the farewell in the rendezvous was even more romantic and repeated several times. Hands were loosened and retaken. In other words, they always left with the hope of meeting once again as soon as possible.

If the reader is acquainted with *Gladys, My Unforgettable Love,* he/she already knows that it was Gladys who declared to the author in a very feminine way that she needed to be his wife rather than his girlfriend. For Antonio this was the moment he had to make-up his mind and decide whether to marry her. He had several difficult decisions to face – some of which were inherent to the economic incompetence of Cuban socialism like the shortage of housing for newlyweds to live independently. Antonio had to face his mother's rejection of Gladys because she was not white, besides the difficult situation with his children's mother, his children's feeble acceptance of their stepmother, as well as Antonio's difficult financial situation – his first financial requirement being his children's alimony – and the need to find a second job to supplement his salary as university professor. In summary, there were many obstacles to be overcome in making his happiness complete with a second marriage. Nonetheless, Antonio was already convinced that Gladys was the woman in his life, and he made the decision to marry her. He realized that he could not live without her. In the meantime, they were happy together and got married ten months after their first rendezvous.

By squeezing themselves in a very small service room in Antonio's sister's home, the newlyweds partially solved their housing situation. Sometime afterwards a disagreement between Antonio and his sister rendered the couple homeless on a warm summer night in Havana. The silver lining of this situation was that Antonio could live with Gladys' family, whose incredibly beneficial togetherness had a very favorable impact on him because he could experience first-hand the roots of Gladys' exceptionalism!

The couple now lived in a home where respect and consideration were displayed every day, where a lady sitting in a wheelchair assumed the financial responsibility of a home, in which everyone had his/her place, where a wallet full of money could be temporarily placed on a table and nobody ever dared taking it. The home in which everybody was respected by – and respectful to – others, where everyone could place something to eat in the refrigerator, knowing that nobody would take it without asking for permission, where if any member of the family was having financial difficulties, he/she would be helped by the rest of the family. In this place lies or betrayals were not accepted or even conceived. To speak in a low voice was the rule for men and women. Although he could only wear underclothes inside the room assigned to them and although sexual relations were done in silence, the joy he experienced in the two years they lived with Gladys' family incomparably outweighed the small limitations faced as the only male now living in the family house. Curiously enough, he was not allowed to do the dishes, or any task normally assigned to women; consequently, Gladys was overloaded with the chores.

To him, it became clear that the reason for Gladys' great performance could be found in the roots of her family's home, characterized by compassion and respect for others. Gladys was very different from every other lady, whom the author had met so far. Therefore, in an almost automatic way, some of the social deficiencies of his character started to be modified or sometimes substituted by more considerate, respectable, and empathetic actions.

<u>Siria Pita's talents start to intertwine with Gladys'.</u>

From a symbolic standpoint, Siria Pita's talents started to mix with Gladys' empathy. Both ladies were tenacious and fought for their rights and convictions.

Although Siria offered some resistance, she gradually started to accept Gladys' race. Her visits to the aunts' farm, and Gladys' monolithic unconditional love for the author were having a positive effect on his mother. Siria had to recognize that kindness, respect, and education – which she thought were virtues exclusive to white people – were perfectly accessible to other races as well. Gladys did not have any inconvenience in establishing a respectful relationship with Siria, and little by little the resistance became acceptance.

There is an outstanding event that took place in Cuba during the Special Period and at a time when the author was suffering pneumonia. It was difficult – quite difficult, almost impossible – to purchase a piece of meat in Cuba even to feed a sick person. It was mid-1992 when Fidel Castro's inflexibility did not allow the population to buy food or anything else from farmers when they were not available at the governmental stores. Under these conditions Gladys was forced to break the "law" to save the author's life. She managed to get transportation to the countryside to buy a piece of pork meat. Siria also wanted to contribute to his rehabilitation by cutting a heavy bunch of bananas from her backyard. At the time she was 82 years old, and she boarded two buses full of people, before she could get to his home with the heavy load. (By the way my home occupied part of the fifth floor of an apartment building without elevators). She had to walk two large blocks from Fifth Avenue. Gladys saw her from the balcony and rushed down the stairs to meet and help her. Finally, both got to the fifth floor, where he was waiting for their arrival. When both women arrived, they hugged each other. Gladys couldn't control her emotions while thanking Siria for her prowess. This scene materialized in front of him with a big hug. He was very happy to witness their mutual affection. The racial prejudice had been definitively overcome.

Back in 1993 when he was chosen to work as a research leader about environmental economics in Mexico, he went alone – according to the University of Havana's policy for faculty teaching abroad during the early 1990s – and Gladys stayed in Havana during the so-called Special Period which was characterized by an acute scarcity of food, transportation, and moral and physical values. Hunger and unsatisfied simple needs motivated people to fight for a piece of bread. In December of the same year, he returned to Cuba for two weeks, during which he could mitigate his families' elementary needs. He returned to Mexico and kept on working alone until the end of the academic year, during which the Mexican university renewed his contract for a second year. He only gave one condition to the Mexican institution – he needed to get Gladys out of Cuba. So, Gladys arrived in Merida on July 20th, 1994. Upon Gladys' arrival, he noticed how much her health had deteriorated in six months. It was to the point that he had a hard time identifying her among the passengers of her flight. When he hugged her, she whispered in his ear a phrase that surprised him. She told him, "Antonio, I am not going back to Cuba, never again. I have suffered tremendously, and I am fed up with so much falsehood and propaganda." He still was not ready to defect.

He was about to finish his second year in Mexico when the Merida Technological Institute was approved by the Mexican Research Institute to grant a scholarship in his name from April 1995 to March 1996. When he contacted the University of Havana for approval of his third year in Mexico – he had to be approved by the Communist Party of both the University and the Ministry of Higher Education. He was informed of their approval and started his third contract. Everything was going very well until the end of the first quarter when he received news from Cuba that his mother had gotten seriously ill. He felt the need to return to Cuba for a week to accompany her, maybe for the last time. Gladys was shocked to hear his decision and recommended him not to return because she had the hunch that something terrible would happen to him. He did not listen to her advice and arrived in Havana on July 15, 1995, planning to return to Mexico on July 22. According to the procedure established by the International Relations Department of the University of Havana, he delivered his passport with the intention of picking it up two days later. Now, an unexpected and unpleasant surprise – and lack of respect for his prestige as a professor – took place. They did not return his passport to him arguing that – according to a recent decision from the Ministry of Higher Education – no Cuban professor could stay abroad for more than two years. He already was in his third year – something previously approved by them, so he couldn't return to Mexico, and Gladys and he were separated again.

From that very moment, he was caught between his two big loves. On one hand, his mother saw he was suffering, without any work to do, a time he would have been fully busy in Mexico with ten students he was mentoring in their theses, besides the interesting and useful research he was conducting about environmental economics in Yucatan agriculture, and the agricultural industry at large. His mother grew in him love and responsibility for his work and could not understand how her revolutionary idol – Fidel Castro had presumed to be the hero of fostering and developing education in Cuba – could interrupt and boycott her beloved son. She saw him suffering each Sunday when he spoke with Gladys over the phone.

Gladys stayed in Mexico, restlessly fighting for his return to Mexico. Once per week, each of them went twice to the airports of Havana and Merida to send and to receive letters from each other. In this way she and he were kept abreast of the situation in both countries. Not only tenacity and courage, but also empathy had grown so strongly in Gladys that she was able to persuade strangers who were traveling between Merida and Havana to take letters from her to him and from him to her. Under normal circumstances, Gladys did not like to address strangers… even less foreigners… to ask for their cooperation, but this time, it was necessary for their cause that she overcame her shyness and asked complete strangers for help.

Siria Pita did not know what to do, or how to help her son. Her health had been improving and now her beloved son was being punished for his wish to console her during her illness. So, she felt guilty for his disgrace. Her son had been detached from useful work in Mexico only to be lazy without anything to do in Cuba without students or any type of teaching or research. For Siria it was hard to accept her own incorrect notions about Fidel Castro and to admit that his behavior was becoming irrational. She preferred not to talk about the situation; while the author only limited himself to underlining his unjustified loneliness, which he tried to take out of his mind by writing a book, which he would be publishing in Mexico, if he ever got back.

One of the Sundays, Gladys let him know that she had unfairly and without justification been declared "illegal" following instructions from the Cuban Consulate in Merida.

The purpose of her "illegality" was that Cuba wanted to have Gladys back in the country, in which case all his hopes to leave the country would have gone astray. When the author heard Gladys' trembling voice on the phone, and feeling impotent to do anything to help her, he couldn't help sobbing. Siria Pita couldn't bear to see her son crying, especially if his tears were for an injustice done against the woman in his life. She approached him and told him, "Tony, I am so sorry to see what is going on. You love Gladys more than anybody else, and you have been unfairly separated. Look, leave Cuba for good, and do not look back."

He strongly hugged and held his mother in his arms strongly. When he was going to kiss her, she escaped from his arms and told him in a broken voice, "Sorry, if I do not rush to the kitchen right now we would have to eat burnt rice." He stood for some seconds with his arms still open, but with a smile on his face. His mother had just authorized him to defect; consequently, there was no reason at all to stay in Cuba.

4.5 The Interaction Between My Two Loves

"No one should come between you and your spouse. They should come along with you, but not between you."

Ashley McIlwain

"I have a great relationship with my mother-in-law. We're both Lions, and understand each other"

Tori Ovnos

After analyzing the interaction between mother and son, and husband and wife, let us now focus on the interaction between the author's two loves; that is to say, how their talents intersect and complement the other's talents with a combination of tenacity, capacity to overcome obstacles, bravery and a large dose of love and empathy.

Siria Pita – voluntarily or involuntarily – now led him totally towards Gladys' protection. The three of them were irremediably separated by political differences, but strong links of love were intertwined between the three of them. Two months after Siria Pita had given to her son the authorization to defect, Antonio went back to Mexico and joined his life once again to Gladys'. As husband and wife, they fought to stay in Mexico, and together united their destinies, in the wills to go ahead, and to achieve the American dream. They became American citizens in 2004.

Siria Pita stayed in Cuba, unable to leave the island in which Antonio and Gladys were born. Two months after their arrival, they could talk to her over the phone. Their last call took place on December 24th, 1997, while the Cuban family was "celebrating" Christmas with his three siblings and their families. He sent her many kisses while telling her that he loved her very much. She kept asking when she was going to see him again, and he answered as soon as possible. On several occasions he told her that he loved her very much and she responded in the same terms.

Three nights after this conversation, he was participating in a scientific event in Chicago, and when he went to the men's room a quiet and internal voice told me, "Siria Pita has just expired". The following day, his son called him and confirmed that his mother had died the previous night. He cried, as men do, in the shadows to hide his pain. He wouldn't be able to hear her voice or talk to her again. Nonetheless, he had the privilege and satisfaction to have made her happy shortly before she had gone.

After, that he only had Gladys until October 5th, 2015, when she died in his arms under his kisses and his love songs.

A famous phrase taken from José Martí – the indisputable apostle of Cuban liberty – reads this: "Death is not true when the deceased successfully achieved the purpose of his life."

Both are gone, but they are still alive in the author with the talents that they bestowed – and helped to develop – in him.

They come back to life when he follows their wise teachings, when he can stand up after a fall, when he reaches a goal, when – by means of empathy – he can satisfactorily solve difficult problems or issues and he receives gratefulness and comfort, when he gives hope to somebody who appears to be lost, when – in exchange for solidarity and support – he is blessed with a smile.

Food for thought

Which ones of the talents have played the most important role in the reconciliation between mother and wife?

Despite their different original political, economic, social, and educational environments, which – in the readers' opinion – was one of the most important reasons for the successful ending of this real-life story?

Has the man in the trio played a primary, secondary, or tertiary role in the appeasement between his big true loves?

The readers are asked to deduct which were the main crucial economic, political, and social moments of this triple propitiation.

May the Lord bless this author's two big loves!

Antonio Evaristo Morales-Pita, PhD has served as Adjunct Faculty of Economics at DePaul University, Chicago, from 1999 to 2019, and as Invited Assistant Professor of International Political Economy from 2009 to 2016. Over the last forty-two years, he has been working as an educator in Cuban, Mexican and American universities. He is the author of eight books and of more than 200 papers related to the application of mathematical models to economics, to the economic evaluation and solution of environmental problems, to the teaching of economics, and international political economy.

He is recipient of the Media Star 2008 and Excellence in Teaching Award 2007 Excellence at DePaul University, first part-time professor recipient of this award at the College of Commerce since its inception more than twenty years ago, of the Cátedra Patrimonial de CONACyT 2005–2006 grant at the Merida's Institute of Technology, Yucatán, Mexico (first Cuban professor to receive this award at the University of Havana), and of awards as outstanding professor and researcher granted by the Cuban Higher Education System, the Cuban Academy of Sciences, the Union of University Professors of Cuba and the University of Havana.

For more information on scheduling Dr Morales-Pita for talks about this book, as well as topics such as enhancing parents' participation and involvement in their children's success in school or college, ways of developing tenacity in students, parents, and teachers, and having a successful and optimistic life after retirement, please contact:

Dr Antonio Morales-Pita
Phone (773) 939-7279
E-mail: amoralespita1@gmail.com